D1573184

PAUL
VON
HINDENBURG

PAUL
VON
HINDENBURG

Russell A. Berman

CHELSEA HOUSE PUBLISHERS
NEW YORK
NEW HAVEN   PHILADELPHIA

EDITOR-IN-CHIEF: Nancy Toff
EXECUTIVE EDITOR: Remmel T. Nunn
MANAGING EDITOR: Karyn Gullen Browne
COPY CHIEF: Perry Scott King
ART DIRECTOR: Giannella Garrett
PICTURE EDITOR: Elizabeth Terhune

Staff for PAUL VON HINDENBURG:

SENIOR EDITOR: John W. Selfridge
ASSISTANT EDITORS: Maria Behan, Pierre Hauser, Kathleen McDermott, Bert Yaeger
COPY EDITORS: Gillian Bucky, Sean Dolan
DESIGN ASSISTANT: Jill Goldreyer
PICTURE RESEARCH: Sarah Kirshner
LAYOUT: Carol McDougall
PRODUCTION COORDINATOR: Alma Rodriguez
PRODUCTION ASSISTANT: Karen Dreste
COVER ILLUSTRATION: Michael Garland

CREATIVE DIRECTOR: Harold Steinberg

039340 ✓

16.95

Frontispiece courtesy of the German Information Center

First Printing

Library of Congress Cataloging in Publication Data

Berman, Russell A., PAUL VON HINDENBURG

(World leaders past & present)
Bibliography: p.
Includes index.
1. Hindenburg, Paul von, 1847–1934—Juvenile literature.
2. Presidents—Germany—Biography—Juvenile literature.
3. Germany—History—1871–   —Juvenile literature.
I. Title. II. Series.
DD231.H5B47   1987   943.085'092'4 [B]   86-29907

ISBN 0-87754-532-4

Contents

CHELSEA HOUSE PUBLISHERS

WORLD LEADERS PAST & PRESENT

ADENAUER
ALEXANDER THE GREAT
MARC ANTONY
KING ARTHUR
ATATÜRK
ATTLEE
BEGIN
BEN-GURION
BISMARCK
LÉON BLUM
BOLÍVAR
CESARE BORGIA
BRANDT
BREZHNEV
CAESAR
CALVIN
CASTRO
CATHERINE THE GREAT
CHARLEMAGNE
CHIANG KAI-SHEK
CHURCHILL
CLEMENCEAU
CLEOPATRA
CORTÉS
CROMWELL
DANTON
DE GAULLE
DE VALERA
DISRAELI
EISENHOWER
ELEANOR OF AQUITAINE
QUEEN ELIZABETH I
FERDINAND AND ISABELLA
FRANCO

FREDERICK THE GREAT
INDIRA GANDHI
MOHANDAS GANDHI
GARIBALDI
GENGHIS KHAN
GLADSTONE
GORBACHEV
HAMMARSKJÖLD
HENRY VIII
HENRY OF NAVARRE
HINDENBURG
HITLER
HO CHI MINH
HUSSEIN
IVAN THE TERRIBLE
ANDREW JACKSON
JEFFERSON
JOAN OF ARC
POPE JOHN XXIII
LYNDON JOHNSON
JUÁREZ
JOHN F. KENNEDY
KENYATTA
KHOMEINI
KHRUSHCHEV
MARTIN LUTHER KING, JR.
KISSINGER
LENIN
LINCOLN
LLOYD GEORGE
LOUIS XIV
LUTHER
JUDAS MACCABEUS
MAO ZEDONG

MARY, QUEEN OF SCOTS
GOLDA MEIR
METTERNICH
MUSSOLINI
NAPOLEON
NASSER
NEHRU
NERO
NICHOLAS II
NIXON
NKRUMAH
PERICLES
PERÓN
QADDAFI
ROBESPIERRE
ELEANOR ROOSEVELT
FRANKLIN D. ROOSEVELT
THEODORE ROOSEVELT
SADAT
STALIN
SUN YAT-SEN
TAMERLANE
THATCHER
TITO
TROTSKY
TRUDEAU
TRUMAN
VICTORIA
WASHINGTON
WEIZMANN
WOODROW WILSON
XERXES
ZHOU ENLAI

ON LEADERSHIP
Arthur M. Schlesinger, jr.

LEADERSHIP, it may be said, is really what makes the world go round. Love no doubt smooths the passage; but love is a private transaction between consenting adults. Leadership is a public transaction with history. The idea of leadership affirms the capacity of individuals to move, inspire, and mobilize masses of people so that they act together in pursuit of an end. Sometimes leadership serves good purposes, sometimes bad; but whether the end is benign or evil, great leaders are those men and women who leave their personal stamp on history.

Now, the very concept of leadership implies the proposition that individuals can make a difference. This proposition has never been universally accepted. From classical times to the present day, eminent thinkers have regarded individuals as no more than the agents and pawns of larger forces, whether the gods and goddesses of the ancient world or, in the modern era, race, class, nation, the dialectic, the will of the people, the spirit of the times, history itself. Against such forces, the individual dwindles into insignificance.

So contends the thesis of historical determinism. Tolstoy's great novel *War and Peace* offers a famous statement of the case. Why, Tolstoy asked, did millions of men in the Napoleonic wars, denying their human feelings and their common sense, move back and forth across Europe slaughtering their fellows? "The war," Tolstoy answered, "was bound to happen simply because it was bound to happen." All prior history predetermined it. As for leaders, they, Tolstoy said, "are but the labels that serve to give a name to an end and, like labels, they have the least possible connection with the event." The greater the leader, "the more conspicuous the inevitability and the predestination of every act he commits." The leader, said Tolstoy, is "the slave of history."

Determinism takes many forms. Marxism is the determinism of class. Nazism the determinism of race. But the idea of men and women as the slaves of history runs athwart the deepest human instincts. Rigid determinism abolishes the idea of human freedom—

the assumption of free choice that underlies every move we make, every word we speak, every thought we think. It abolishes the idea of human responsibility, since it is manifestly unfair to reward or punish people for actions that are by definition beyond their control. No one can live consistently by any deterministic creed. The Marxist states prove this themselves by their extreme susceptibility to the cult of leadership.

More than that, history refutes the idea that individuals make no difference. In December 1931 a British politician crossing Park Avenue in New York City between 76th and 77th Streets around 10:30 P.M. looked in the wrong direction and was knocked down by an automobile—a moment, he later recalled, of a man aghast, a world aglare: "I do not understand why I was not broken like an eggshell or squashed like a gooseberry." Fourteen months later an American politician, sitting in an open car in Miami, Florida, was fired on by an assassin; the man beside him was hit. Those who believe that individuals make no difference to history might well ponder whether the next two decades would have been the same had Mario Constasino's car killed Winston Churchill in 1931 and Giuseppe Zangara's bullet killed Franklin Roosevelt in 1933. Suppose, in addition, that Adolf Hitler had been killed in the street fighting during the Munich *Putsch* of 1923 and that Lenin had died of typhus during World War I. What would the 20th century be like now?

For better or for worse, individuals do make a difference. "The notion that a people can run itself and its affairs anonymously," wrote the philosopher William James, "is now well known to be the silliest of absurdities. Mankind does nothing save through initiatives on the part of inventors, great or small, and imitation by the rest of us—these are the sole factors in human progress. Individuals of genius show the way, and set the patterns, which common people then adopt and follow."

Leadership, James suggests, means leadership in thought as well as in action. In the long run, leaders in thought may well make the greater difference to the world. But, as Woodrow Wilson once said, "Those only are leaders of men, in the general eye, who lead in action. . . . It is at their hands that new thought gets its translation into the crude language of deeds." Leaders in thought often invent in solitude and obscurity, leaving to later generations the tasks of imitation. Leaders in action—the leaders portrayed in this series—have to be effective in their own time.

And they cannot be effective by themselves. They must act in response to the rhythms of their age. Their genius must be adapted, in a phrase of William James's, "to the receptivities of the moment." Leaders are useless without followers. "There goes the mob," said the French politician hearing a clamor in the streets. "I am their leader. I must follow them." Great leaders turn the inchoate emotions of the mob to purposes of their own. They seize on the opportunities of their time, the hopes, fears, frustrations, crises, potentialities. They succeed when events have prepared the way for them, when the community is awaiting to be aroused, when they can provide the clarifying and organizing ideas. Leadership ignites the circuit between the individual and the mass and thereby alters history.

It may alter history for better or for worse. Leaders have been responsible for the most extravagant follies and most monstrous crimes that have beset suffering humanity. They have also been vital in such gains as humanity has made in individual freedom, religious and racial tolerance, social justice and respect for human rights.

There is no sure way to tell in advance who is going to lead for good and who for evil. But a glance at the gallery of men and women in *World Leaders—Past and Present* suggests some useful tests.

One test is this: do leaders lead by force or by persuasion? By command or by consent? Through most of history leadership was exercised by the divine right of authority. The duty of followers was to defer and to obey. "Theirs not to reason why,/ Theirs but to do and die." On occasion, as with the so-called "enlightened despots" of the 18th century in Europe, absolutist leadership was animated by humane purposes. More often, absolutism nourished the passion for domination, land, gold and conquest and resulted in tyranny.

The great revolution of modern times has been the revolution of equality. The idea that all people should be equal in their legal condition has undermined the old structure of authority, hierarchy and deference. The revolution of equality has had two contrary effects on the nature of leadership. For equality, as Alexis de Tocqueville pointed out in his great study *Democracy in America*, might mean equality in servitude as well as equality in freedom.

"I know of only two methods of establishing equality in the political world," Tocqueville wrote. "Rights must be given to every citizen, or none at all to anyone . . . save one, who is the master of all." There was no middle ground "between the sovereignty of all and the absolute power of one man." In his astonishing prediction of 20th-century totalitarian dictatorship, Tocqueville explained how the revolution of equality could lead to the *"Führerprinzip"* and more terrible absolutism than the world had ever known.

But when rights are given to every citizen and the sovereignty of all is established, the problem of leadership takes a new form, becomes more exacting than ever before. It is easy to issue commands and enforce them by the rope and the stake, the concentration camp and the *gulag.* It is much harder to use argument and achievement to overcome opposition and win consent. The Founding Fathers of the United States understood the difficulty. They believed that history had given them the opportunity to decide, as Alexander Hamilton wrote in the first Federalist Paper, whether men are indeed capable of basing government on "reflection and choice, or whether they are forever destined to depend . . . on accident and force."

Government by reflection and choice called for a new style of leadership and a new quality of followership. It required leaders to be responsive to popular concerns, and it required followers to be active and informed participants in the process. Democracy does not eliminate emotion from politics; sometimes it fosters demagoguery; but it is confident that, as the greatest of democratic leaders put it, you cannot fool all of the people all of the time. It measures leadership by results and retires those who overreach or falter or fail.

It is true that in the long run despots are measured by results too. But they can postpone the day of judgment, sometimes indefinitely, and in the meantime they can do infinite harm. It is also true that democracy is no guarantee of virtue and intelligence in government, for the voice of the people is not necessarily the voice of God. But democracy, by assuring the right of opposition, offers built-in resistance to the evils inherent in absolutism. As the theologian Reinhold Niebuhr summed it up, "Man's capacity for justice makes democracy possible, but man's inclination to injustice makes democracy necessary."

A second test for leadership is the end for which power is sought. When leaders have as their goal the supremacy of a master race or the promotion of totalitarian revolution or the acquisition and exploitation of colonies or the protection of greed and privilege or the preservation of personal power, it is likely that their leadership will do little to advance the cause of humanity. When their goal is the abolition of slavery, the liberation of women, the enlargement of opportunity for the poor and powerless, the extension of equal rights to racial minorities, the defense of the freedoms of expression and opposition, it is likely that their leadership will increase the sum of human liberty and welfare.

Leaders have done great harm to the world. They have also conferred great benefits. You will find both sorts in this series. Even "good" leaders must be regarded with a certain wariness. Leaders are not demigods; they put on their trousers one leg after another just like ordinary mortals. No leader is infallible, and every leader needs to be reminded of this at regular intervals. Irreverence irritates leaders but is their salvation. Unquestioning submission corrupts leaders and demands followers. Making a cult of a leader is always a mistake. Fortunately hero worship generates its own antidote. "Every hero," said Emerson, "becomes a bore at last."

The signal benefit the great leaders confer is to embolden the rest of us to live according to our own best selves, to be active, insistent, and resolute in affirming our own sense of things. For great leaders attest to the reality of human freedom against the supposed inevitabilities of history. And they attest to the wisdom and power that may lie within the most unlikely of us, which is why Abraham Lincoln remains the supreme example of great leadership. A great leader, said Emerson, exhibits new possibilities to all humanity. "We feed on genius. . . . Great men exist that there may be greater men."

Great leaders, in short, justify themselves by emancipating and empowering their followers. So humanity struggles to master its destiny, remembering with Alexis de Tocqueville: "It is true that around every man a fatal circle is traced beyond which he cannot pass; but within the wide verge of that circle he is powerful and free; as it is with man, so with communities."

1

The Martial Tradition

Dawn was but a few hours away. In the early-morning darkness on August 23, 1914, the German city of Hanover slept. Yet Europe was at war. World War I, the "Great War," had broken out on August 1. Standing motionless, waiting on the train platform, was a large, somewhat stout man. His silent, dignified bearing told that he had been a soldier for most of his 66 years. He glanced at his pocket watch. If he was nervous, nothing in his manner showed it. It was only minutes before a special train would arrive to take him to East Prussia (now part of Poland and the Soviet Union). There an army waited for him to take command. Paul von Hindenburg was answering a call to duty issued by Germany's *Kaiser*, or emperor, Wilhelm II. The previous day, a telegram had arrived for him from the kaiser, promoting him to colonel general and commander in chief of the troops fighting Russia. Was he prepared to return to active service? "Am ready" was Hindenburg's immediate reply.

Three years earlier Hindenburg had retired from the army as a commander general. By that time he had spent 46 years in the army. During his retirement he had grown to miss military life. The quiet

The German soul is opposed to the pacifist ideal of civilization, for is not peace an element of civil corruption?
—THOMAS MANN
German novelist

Paul von Hindenburg had retired as a commander general from the German army in 1911. In August 1914, during World War I, he was promoted to colonel general by the German *Kaiser* (emperor) and made commander of German forces fighting Russian invaders in East Prussia — Hindenburg's home province. His victories there made him a hero to his countrymen.

years had made him restless. Now his future, and that of Germany, had changed literally overnight. The fame he was about to win would make him a national hero. His reputation would carry over into the tumultuous mid-1920s, when Germany was searching for a leader who would restore confidence during the difficult postwar period.

With a hiss of steam, the train pulled into the station at 3:00 A.M. The new commander in chief of the German Eighth Army saw another officer in a field-gray uniform emerge from one of the train's two cars. This was the general who, according to the kaiser's message, was named to serve as Hindenburg's chief of staff: Major General Erich von Ludendorff. Ludendorff was a respected general

The train station (with clock) near the Ernst-August-Platz in Hanover, Germany, where Hindenburg boarded a train on August 23, 1914, that took him and his second in command, Erich von Ludendorff, to East Prussia. There, they led a counteroffensive against the Russian army.

who had distinguished himself at Liège, where German troops, on their way through Belgium to attack France, captured a fortress early in August 1914. He saluted Hindenburg smartly. Returning the salute, Hindenburg joined him on board the train. Ludendorff, an excitable, often difficult man, began to explain his strategy. He said that the battle plan he was describing had already been sent in advance to the front. Hindenburg listened. Even during the heat of battle, or when he had suffered the worst punishments as a young cadet in military school, Hindenburg remained calm. As Ludendorff spoke, it seemed that there was little for Hindenburg to say. He was delighted to find that he agreed with virtually everything the major general said. He and Ludendorff would eventually oversee all German battle plans for the duration of the war.

Their train steamed eastward, on to the German army headquarters in Marienburg (now Malbork, Poland), where Hindenburg had orders to replace Lieutenant General Max von Prittwitz. The German war effort against Russia was faltering. Under Prittwitz the Germans had already been beaten at the Battle of Gumbinnen (now the Soviet city of Gusev), where Russian General Pavel Rennenkampf's huge First Army had overwhelmed German attempts to stop it. Although the Russians had a two-to-one advantage in numbers, the Germans had been confident of their fighting superiority. They were

In August 1914 German troops leave the fighting in France and proceed to East Prussia to help battle the Russian army. Hindenburg and Ludendorff smashed the Russian forces at the Battle of Tannenberg without these reinforcements, which were needed against France and Great Britain, Russia's allies.

15

Lieutenant General Erich von Ludendorff studies a map during the fighting against the huge Russian army on the eastern front. After capturing a key fortress at Liège, Belgium, early in August, he was quickly appointed Hindenburg's chief of staff; his strategic brilliance played a vital role in driving back the poorly led Russian army.

shocked now that the Russians were advancing in East Prussia and taking German territory. The kaiser was putting his trust in Hindenburg and Ludendorff to defeat the Russians. Ludendorff was known to be brilliant and brave, but he had a fiery temper and was also prone to worry. Hindenburg, on the other hand, never panicked. He was careful, deliberate, and coolheaded. He swiftly understood when Ludendorff had found a solution that would outwit the enemy and win battles. When Ludendorff's temper flared, Hindenburg was able to restrain him.

Their mutual respect and ability to see the other's point of view would be tested to the limit by the tensions of the biggest war ever fought up until that time. Ludendorff recalled, however, that in the ensuing battles, they "worked together in deepest harmony, as one man." On the day they met and rode the train to the eastern front, Hindenburg issued an order of his own. It said: "We will trust one another and do our duty together." In his autobiography, *Aus meinem Leben (Out of My Life)*, published in 1920, Hindenburg looked back on their association: "We met in our thoughts as in our actions, and the words of the one were often only the expression and thoughts and feelings of the other. I regarded it as one of my highest duties as soon as I recognized the merit of General Ludendorff to leave a clear path, or if necessary to clear the way [for Ludendorff's thinking] and untiring industry."

To put German forces on the offensive and send the giant Russian army fleeing from East Prussia was the German commanders' first priority. Prittwitz, with another top officer, had created a set of plans for such an offensive, yet they had hesitated. Possibly the most important difference between Ludendorff's plan and that of his immediate predecessors was that Ludendorff's would be put into action. Hindenburg and Ludendorff spent little time discussing what needed to be done to reverse the situation against General Rennenkampf and General Aleksandr Samsonov, whose armies were then marching west at a pace of 16 miles a day. Hindenburg signed the order to mobilize the German coun-

terattack against the approaching Russians on August 25.

Paul Ludwig Hans Anton von Beneckendorff und von Hindenburg was born on October 2, 1847, in Posen, East Prussia (now Poznan, Poland). His father, Robert, was an officer in the Prussian army and came from a long line of soldiers. Hindenburg was born a *Junker*, a member of the Prussian landowning nobility. Its origin dates to the time of the feudal princes and warlords who, during the Middle Ages, commanded the loyalty of the people who lived on their land. Hindenburg's family claimed that their name dated to the 13th century. East Prussia had once been the domain of warriors, the Teutonic Knights, who had settled the region at this time. Although their small empire was destroyed during the 15th century, their descendants became the Prussian aristocracy. From its foundation as a duchy in the 16th century, Prussia had gradually grown into a kingdom that stretched from the Elbe River in the west to the Neman River on the Russian border.

Paul's father was born in 1816 and attended a wealthy school for the sons of Junkers in Königsberg (now Kaliningrad in the Soviet Union). His

Russian troops take up position in an East Prussian forest. German forces under General Max von Prittwitz were unable to check the advancing Russians at the Battle of Gumbinnen. But by the fall of 1914 the Russians had absorbed several devastating defeats. They suffered as much from hunger as from superior German planning.

> *It is necessary that our civilization should build its temple on mountains of corpses, on an ocean of tears, and on the death cries of men without number.*
> —COUNT GOTTLIEB VON HAESELER
> Prussian officer

birth occurred shortly after the Prussian War of Liberation, when Prussia had helped to defeat the French conqueror Emperor Napoleon Bonaparte. In 1807 Friedrich Wilhelm III, the Prussian king, had been forced to surrender extensive areas to Napoleon. By 1815 Napoleon's forces had been defeated, and Prussia regained the previously surrendered areas of western Pomerania, part of Saxony, Westphalia, and the Rhineland.

As a child, Hindenburg moved frequently, since his father served at various outposts in towns such as Posen, Pinne, Cologne, and Glogau. To Paul's mother, Louisa, the daughter of a physician, and his father, a lieutenant and adjutant, there never was any doubt that their eldest son was bound for a career in the army. He would follow automatically in the footsteps of the troops constantly marching in the courtyards and training fields. His career had been decided virtually at birth.

Paul, his two younger brothers, and his sister traveled from garrison to garrison with their parents and grew up with the constant din of marching and the sight of troops parading nearby. The only time he was away from the dust and shouting of the parade grounds was when the family lived in the small village of Pinne. The Hindenburgs' house there had a garden and a small stream. In this environment he spent some of the happiest times of his childhood.

Prussia's military tradition, however, was all around him as a small boy. He recalled how a nurse who had participated in the Napoleonic Wars quieted the children by shouting, "Don't speak in the ranks." Another important link with Prussia's past was his grandfather, Otto Ludwig, who died when Paul was 16 years old. Neudeck, his grandparents' estate in the area east of the Elbe River, had been taken over by the French during the war with Napoleon. In 1863, when Robert retired from the military, Paul lived at Neudeck with his grandparents. For the rest of his life he would consider this house his ancestral home. Neudeck and a second estate had actually been awarded to one of Hindenburg's ancestors for his service in the War of the Austrian

Succession (1740–48). In a letter thanking the Prussian King Frederick the Great (Frederick II), the humble soldier wrote, "What am I, Lord, and what is my family that you have caused us to rise in this way?"

One event that made a lifelong impression on him was meeting an elderly gardener at his grandparents' estate. The old man told him stories of a bygone age when the 18th-century Prussian King Frederick the Great built the Prussian legal system and made the state into an important and respected European power. The king had gained much territory as well as military glory in the War of the Austrian Succession. The gardener, who had been in the army personally commanded by Frederick, told the young Hindenburg about this legendary leader. He recalled later that this conversation made him feel that he was connected to this period and what it stood for in history.

Frederick died in 1786. The defeats inflicted on the Prussian armies by Napoleon in 1806 and 1807

The young cadet Paul von Hindenburg (standing, far right) poses with his father, Robert, his mother, Louisa (center, seated), his younger sister, and two brothers. Robert, a *Junker*, or member of the Prussian nobility, was an officer in the Prussian army when Paul was born on October 2, 1847.

Artisans, such as this German toolmaker and cabinetmaker, were threatened by modern industry during the mid-19th century. Industrial workers and artisans in France began the Revolution of 1848, which spread to Germany. Worker unrest during this period was never discussed by Hindenburg's Junker family.

exposed weaknesses within the state and brought a sudden clamoring for improvements in the way Prussia was governed. When Prussia was partitioned by Napoleon's forces, there were those who felt reforms were urgently needed in order to "reconstruct" the state. Without Frederick the Great's strength of personality and leadership, Prussia could not survive as it had unless significant adjustments were made. Only reforms would ensure the people's continued support for the Prussian state. A member of the aristocracy who was influenced by the French Revolution (1789–99) began instituting these reforms. Municipal self-government was established, and the peasants, called serfs, were freed from their feudal owners. Industry was also encouraged, and a new class — the middle class — and its values began to become a major influence on Prussian society.

Despite the Prussian devotion to custom and avoidance of change, even his grandfather had once broken with tradition. The Junkers were expected to marry within their own class. Otto Ludwig, however, allowed one of his daughters to marry a commoner, someone outside the aristocracy. Frederick the Great had previously decreed that such marriages could be permitted, but he was extremely critical of Prussian officers who married members of the middle class. A Prussian officer requesting permission for one of his troops who wished to marry a woman from this class was told by the king to discourage "such alliances."

The year Hindenburg was born, hungry citizens had rioted in the streets of Berlin. This period of unrest was called the "potato revolution." The year after his birth, the industrial workers in France had begun a revolution that quickly spread to Germany. In Germany, industrialization had failed to keep pace with the number of workers in need of employment in factories. Artisans who owned their own tools and made their own goods also suffered due to the enormous economic changes taking place in Europe. Meanwhile, a young philosopher and economist named Karl Marx was the editor of a newspaper called the *Neue Rheinische Zeitung*, in which this important "social question," as it was called, was constantly discussed. Marx believed that capitalism, the system of private ownership, would be overthrown by the working class, or "proletariat." They would then establish socialism, the system of collective ownership, and, eventually, a society without classes. Workers began to organize their own councils and congresses.

In March that same year, Polish rebels, whom the Prussians regarded as their enemies, tried to take over the province of Posen. Hindenburg's father led a Prussian regiment against the revolt. When it seemed that the Poles had conquered the city of Posen, their commanding general ordered that all citizens, including Prussians, place a light in their windows in honor of this victory. Hindenburg's mother did as she was ordered, but, coincidentally, the prince of Prussia's birthday fell on that same day, and so she told herself that this was the real reason for her putting the light in the window.

Hindenburg's family never discussed the socialist revolutionaries of 1848, even though the revolt in Germany proved a failure and quickly collapsed. For the rest of his life Hindenburg was deeply opposed to all forms of revolution. He also was suspicious of democracy. Hostile to change, the Prussian military believed that whatever caused mass unrest would soon fade away. If it did not, then any rebelliousness should be suppressed. At an early age Hindenburg learned that loyalty to his king was all-important. It was the duty of a soldier.

Hindenburg could not easily accept ideas with which he was not already familiar. He was not flexible in his thinking. His upbringing had been full of military discipline. As a child, he was treated not much differently than any Prussian soldier was treated by his officers. He learned a deep respect for God, for his nation, and for the Prussian king, whom he would meet as a boy in military school. On that day, he and his classmates were so awed they could not speak.

As one demonstrator scrawls "national ownership" on a building wall, rioters fill the streets of Prussia's capital, Berlin, in 1847, the year Hindenburg was born. Known as the "potato revolution," this uprising and the Revolution of 1848 were regarded with contempt by Prussian Junkers, such as Robert von Hindenburg.

2
A Soldier of the Empire

In 1863 Hindenburg was sent to Berlin, the capital of the kingdom of Prussia, where he would complete the last three years of his military schooling and where he would first see the members of the royal family, whom he was sworn to serve. It was also in Berlin that Otto von Bismarck, the Prussian prime minister, was drawing up plans that would sweep the young cadet Hindenburg into battles intended to establish a united German empire.

Within a year of Hindenburg's arrival in Berlin, war broke out: Prussia and Austria, the two major powers in the central European region of German-speaking peoples, were allies against Denmark. The king of Denmark, Christian IX, had violated an earlier agreement by placing under his direct rule two small provinces, Schleswig and Holstein. Most of the inhabitants of these longtime Danish possessions were Germans. The Danish king wanted to absorb Schleswig. Throughout Prussia and Austria, growing German nationalist sentiments demanded the liberation of Schleswig and Holstein from Danish control. The outbreak of war electrified the German people, who regarded the conflict as the first step toward a complete national unification.

> *Becoming a soldier was for me no decision; it was the natural course of events. Whenever, as a youth, I was asked to choose a profession, it was always the military. Serving king and country in uniform was an old tradition in our family.*
> —PAUL VON HINDENBURG

The 18-year-old Hindenburg in 1865, two years after entering military school in Berlin from Wahlstaat cadet school in Silesia — both brutal institutions. Hindenburg regretted not participating in the Prussian war against Denmark in 1864, but in 1866 he was decorated for bravery in the Seven Weeks' War against Austria.

Nowhere was that excitement felt more strongly than among the cadets in Hindenburg's school in Berlin. Hindenburg's classmates remembered the older students who had recently finished their training and who were now doing battle with the enemy. Letters from the front caused the students to envision acts of heroism and dream of glory on the battlefield. For Hindenburg these dreams were mixed with frustration: when would he too be able to leave the classroom behind and have the chance to fight?

Prussia's victory over Denmark in 1864 was the first step in Bismarck's plan to build the German nation piece by piece. This scheme for Germany's expansion and unification was bringing the eager young Hindenburg closer to the day when he would experience war firsthand.

On April 7, 1866, Hindenburg graduated from the Cadet Corps. He was given the rank of second lieutenant and was assigned to the Third Prussian

A marketplace and courtyard in the city of Danzig (now Gdansk, Poland), about 1900. As part of the Third Prussian Guard Regiment, Hindenburg was stationed here in April 1866 before being ordered to Potsdam, near Berlin. The 19-year-old lieutenant would soon fight in the Seven Weeks' War against Austria.

Guard Regiment in Danzig (now the city of Gdansk in Poland).

The alliance of Prussia and Austria had defeated Denmark and gained control of the provinces of Schleswig and Holstein. Very quickly, Bismarck proceeded to turn against his ally Austria, trying to claim the two provinces for Prussia alone. This angered the Austrians as well as some of the smaller German states. Yet this response was just what Bismarck wanted. In fact, he had initiated the annexation of Schleswig and Holstein above all in order to provoke the Austrians and to set off a new war.

In the war with Denmark in 1864, what was considered German territory had been freed from foreign control. But Austria, like Prussia, considered itself to be the true representative of the Germans. Between France in the west and Russia in the east, numerous independent states existed. In many of them, the population was largely German. Others included Poles, Czechs, Hungarians, and other ethnic groups, but they too were ruled over by German-speaking aristocrats. German nationalists looked forward to a single state that would unify all the Germans under one government, but no one knew how that state would come about or what form it would take. Bismarck made it paramount in his plan that the smaller German states, once unified, would be controlled by Prussia. Prussia would not bow to the very states whose unification it was helping to bring about.

Tensions between Austria and Prussia had been mounting since the 18th century. When Germany became unified, either the Prussian king in Berlin or the Austrian emperor in Vienna was bound to dominate the other. If Austria could be excluded from a unified Germany, then no other state could challenge the supremacy of Prussia. Bismarck understood this calculation very well. In 1866 he gambled that the Prussian army would be able to defeat the Austrians in battle.

Stationed in Danzig in April, Second Lieutenant Hindenburg was transferred with his regiment to Potsdam, near Berlin. Preparations for the impending military confrontation were under way, and the

Prince Otto von Bismarck of Prussia, the "Iron Chancellor," was the 19th-century Junker statesman who forged a unified empire from many separate German states. Hindenburg fought in Bismarck's wars against Austria and France but was unconcerned about the conflicts' political significance.

Prussian King Wilhelm I (later, emperor of Germany) leads the pursuit of the broken Austrian army at the Battle of Königgrätz on July 3, 1866, where the young Hindenburg fought. Days earlier, the new lieutenant experienced his first battle at Soor, where the brilliant Prussian King Frederick the Great also had defeated Austria in 1745.

regiment was expanded. The war with Austria would be known as the Seven Weeks' War. When fighting began, the regiment marched through the southeastern Prussian province of Silesia and into Bohemia, advancing into Austrian territory. In the Battle of Soor, on June 28, Hindenburg got his first taste of war. Here, as Hindenburg was well aware, the celebrated Prussian King Frederick the Great had defeated the Austrians in 1745, inflicting heavy casualties on the larger Austrian army. Because Frederick had been victorious here, for Hindenburg and other Prussian soldiers this battleground was almost sacred.

The battle resulted in a quick victory against the Austrians. The next day Hindenburg was confronted with war's terrible harvest when he had to search the battlefield for the dead and oversee their burials. Later, he was assigned to accompany a convoy of Austrian prisoners of war to a nearby place of detainment. Yet the stark realities of war — killing, injury, the shock of defeat — made little impression on Hindenburg. His enthusiasm was in no way dampened. Unshaken, he hurried to catch up with his regiment, which had continued marching forward.

Hindenburg arrived back at the front just in time to participate in the Battle of Königgrätz (also known as Sadowa) on July 3, 1866. This was the decisive battle of the war between Prussia and Austria. The Prussian victory guaranteed the exclusion of Austria from a unified Germany; it guaranteed that, when formed, the new German state would be under Prussian control.

Königgrätz was a bloody and savage battle. Although it was the height of summer, rain and fog obscured vision. The crops, standing high in the fields, made mobility difficult. Yet the wheat served as very effective cover for Hindenburg and his men. From their positions in the wheat fields, the Prussian foot soldiers picked off the Austrian cavalrymen. Sitting on horseback and wearing white uniforms, they were easy targets.

Half of the soldiers under Hindenburg's command died at Königgrätz. During the battle he led a charge on an Austrian battery of guns. As he ran, a bullet

At the sound of the first bullets one is overcome by a certain enthusiasm (the first bullets are always welcomed with a 'Hurrah!' by the troops). Then one says a short prayer, one thinks for a moment of the dear ones at home . . . and then one dashes ahead.
—PAUL VON HINDENBURG
after the Battle of Soor

During the Franco-Prussian War, masterminded by Bismarck to unify Germany, a French officer waves a white flag of surrender at the Battle of Sedan on September 2, 1870. Hindenburg fought at the earlier Battle of Saint-Privat, and later participated in the siege of Paris.

suddenly smashed into his helmet. He was hurled to the ground, unconscious, but the bullet had passed through his helmet, only grazing his scalp. When he came to, several Austrian guns had already been seized by his men. The Prussians had been greatly outnumbered by the Austrians, but by battle's end, the Austrians had lost 40,000 men, the Prussians only 9,000.

Hindenburg kept his punctured helmet and later displayed it proudly on his desk. That helmet was not his only trophy of the battle. Because he commanded the capture of the battery, he was awarded a medal, the Order of the Red Eagle. Barely two months after finishing school, Hindenburg was an experienced soldier, a veteran of a major battle who had been decorated for heroism under fire.

By the time the Seven Weeks' War with Austria ended on August 23, 1866, Hindenburg's regiment had rapidly advanced into southern Austria, 20 miles from the capital city of Vienna. Returning to Berlin, the Prussian soldiers were hailed as heroes as they passed through the Brandenburg Gate, the city's famed victory arch.

Crowds lined the city streets and applauded the victorious troops. Hindenburg cherished that moment. In his eyes these crowds represented the true Germany, patriotic and enthusiastically devoted to the state. The revolutionaries of 1848, who had appeared threatening to his family at Neudeck, seemed to have been replaced by nationalist masses that were loyal to their king.

Hindenburg's regiment was transferred again, this time to Hanover, the capital of the western German kingdom of the same name. The king of Hanover had been allied with Austria. The victorious Prussians deposed him and seized control of his wealth and territory.

While stationed in the former capital city, Hindenburg occasionally felt the anger of the local population, still hostile to the Prussian soldiers it regarded as foreign. Nevertheless, Hindenburg's strong loyalty to Prussia and his commitment to the vision of a unified Germany generally blinded him to these problems. He continued to carry out his duties as a Prussian officer and a Junker. He could not understand that some Germans might have valid reasons to oppose the expansion of the power of the Prussian king, for whom Hindenburg was fighting.

With the defeat of Austria, Prussia grew much stronger and established the North German Confederation, in the German area north of the Main River. In the south, the German states of Bavaria, Baden, and Würtemberg remained independent. Already, in 1866, the southern states had made certain military agreements with Prussia. By the following year certain economic agreements were reached, and Germany was quickly becoming unified. Now Bismarck turned his attention again to another foreign power.

Because of diplomatic quarrels over the vacant Spanish throne, tensions escalated between Prussia and France. France had been the strongest force on the European continent; suddenly it was threat-

Prussian guns shell Paris in 1871 to force a surrender by the Third Republic, whose government resisted Bismarck after French Emperor Napoleon III's defeat at Sedan. Hindenburg's regiment had marched on Paris in September 1870. Leaders of the Third Republic sued for peace in 1871.

ened by the rise of Prussia. On July 19, 1870, a new war, the third in six years, began. The German states all placed their armies under Prussia's command.

By the middle of August, Hindenburg's regiment had marched into eastern France. At first he failed to find any enemy soldiers. Eager to repeat his experiences of 1866, Hindenburg could not hide his disappointment. He did not have to wait much longer. On August 17 the Third Regiment encountered French forces in the Battle of Saint-Privat, which ended in a German victory. Yet it was a costly victory; 17 officers and 304 soldiers in Hindenburg's regiment had died, and many more were wounded.

Saint-Privat was one of the many swift and decisive victories won by the Germans in August, leading to the Battle of Sedan on September 1, 1870. The French army, led by Emperor Napoleon III, surrendered on September 2, and it seemed the war would end in total German victory. But the war went on: as soon as Napoleon III was defeated in the field and taken prisoner, politicians in Paris declared a government, which was called the Third Republic. It began as a provisional government, quickly patched together by the radical Léon Gambetta and the moderate Jules Favre. These new leaders announced that this republic would continue to resist the German invaders. When Favre met with Bismarck on September 18 to discuss the Prussian's demands, Favre told him that France would give up "not an inch of our territory or a stone of our fortresses."

This turn of events gave Bismarck further encouragement. He claimed that Germany must protect Europe from the antiroyalist revolutionaries in the French capital. He annexed the regions of France along the German border, Alsace and Lorraine, and ordered the German armies to press on toward the heart of France.

With his regiment Hindenburg marched onward, and by September 19 he was camped on the outskirts of Paris. He stayed there during the long siege of Paris. Despite the German army's enormous

Workers seize guns during the unrest that divided the Third Republic after the Franco-Prussian War. Revolutionaries influenced by the radical socialist thinkers Karl Marx and Friedrich Engels led the "Paris Commune." Like Bismarck, Hindenburg applauded the suppression of these socialist revolutionaries.

THE BETTMANN ARCHIVE

strength, it was not unstoppable, and so the war continued.

Although revolutionary and republican demands had divided France in the 1860s, the emergency government tried to rally all France against the German invaders. This new regime was intended to defend against the revolutionaries as well as the Germans. Gambetta, the government's minister of the interior, made a dramatic flight in a balloon that carried him out of Paris and flew him safely over German lines to Tours. In that city he formed his own government, aiming to lead the French provinces against the Germans. He recruited volunteers, but they were a ragtag, unprofessional force, often lacking guns and supplies.

While the war between Bismarck's forces and the French Republic wore on, important political issues developed in Germany. What was meant by "Germany" at this time? When the war had begun in the summer of 1870, Prussia led the forces of the North German Confederation, forged by Bismarck, in an

As Bismarck looks on, Prussian King Wilhelm I is proclaimed emperor of the German Empire in the Hall of Mirrors at the Palace of Versailles, near Paris, on January 18, 1871. Hindenburg was hand-picked to represent his regiment at the ceremony that signified German unification.

31

alliance with the southern German states. Although their armies were fighting side by side against the French, they were still independent states. Given the strong patriotic feelings that accompanied the war, the time was ripe to carry out the political unification of Germany. Bismarck had needed to find a cause that was so powerful, so urgent, that the northern and southern states would unite against a common foe. War with France was just the emergency to accomplish this feat.

Paris was still in the hands of the French government, but the German army controlled the nearby palace of Versailles, built by the French King Louis XIV. Hindenburg was sent to Versailles to represent his regiment at an important ceremony that took place in the palace's Hall of Mirrors on January 18, 1871. The king of Prussia, Wilhelm I, was declared the German emperor, whose title of "kaiser" is the German form of the name for the rulers of ancient Rome: "caesar." The new German Empire, or *Reich* (meaning kingdom), included both the North German Confederation as well as the southern states in a unified nation under Prussian leadership. The Austrians, of course, were excluded.

Hindenburg was an eyewitness to the birth of the German Empire. He had fought for that empire at Königgrätz and Saint-Privat, and he would later defend it again in World War I.

Similarly, Hindenburg understood that his loyalty to the emperor of the new Germany could not allow tolerance of democracy. On January 28, 1871, the French provisional government signed an armistice rather than prolong the starvation that gripped Paris during the four-month seige of the city. The Third Republic's National Assembly approved a peace treaty on March 1, 1871, that ceded Alsace and Lorraine to Germany and forced the French to pay a huge indemnity. Outraged by the surrender terms, bitter about the long months of hunger inflicted by the Prussian siege, and dissatisfied with the National Assembly, Paris's radicals declared their own government on March 26. This was the "Paris Commune." Stationed outside of Paris, Hindenburg was able to observe the insurrection in the city.

Anarchists, democrats, and socialists of the Paris Commune fought against the moderate leadership of the new republic. Eventually they were defeated in a bloody attack by the troops of the French government, who received support from the German army outside the city. Twenty thousand revolutionaries were killed. Many people suspected of participating in the Commune were executed without trial.

Hindenburg applauded the defeat of the Paris Commune. Once established, the new German Empire was immediately hostile to any popular resistance. Bismarck's government was not sympathetic to supporters of democracy, even moderate ones. Bismarck had a great distaste for the provisional government. He much preferred his old foe Emperor Napoleon III to leaders such as Favre and Gambetta. The government Bismarck headed was an autocracy, and he was suspicious of parliamentary decision-making and democracy. Germany, after all, had been unified not by revolution from below but by Bismarck's policies from above.

Hindenburg had not been taught — nor was he expected — to appreciate the complex issues that underlay the wars and the uprisings that were occur-

The various types of cavalrymen and foot soldiers that comprised the Prussian army during the Franco-Prussian War. Hindenburg was an infantryman. Suspicious of democracy and obedient to Germany's emperor, he seldom pondered the political reasons for the wars he fought in.

UPI/BETTMANN NEWSPHOTOS

Hindenburg at age 31 was a captain in the German army. After the Franco-Prussian War accomplished German unification in 1871, Hindenburg returned to Hanover and later enrolled in the Military Academy in Berlin. In 1878 he was appointed to the army's general staff.

ring. He understood whose side he was to fight on, and it was natural for him to rejoice when that side was victorious or when the enemy was foiled. But his mind was not curious beyond this point. This lack of curiosity had marked his character since childhood. When looking back on the Prussian war against Denmark, in which he regretted not having participated, he wrote: "We did not bother or conjure our brains about the political reasons which led to this war."

Coming home from the war in France, Hindenburg settled again in Hanover until he entered the Military Academy in Berlin in 1873. He took advanced military studies in order to promote his career and move up through the ranks of the German army. Living in Berlin also brought him into contact with influential politicians and members of the imperial court.

When Hindenburg graduated from the Military Academy, he returned once again to Hanover. In 1878 he was promoted to the general staff of the army, and during the next two and a half decades he held increasingly important positions in different parts of Germany: Stettin (now Szczecin in Poland), Königsberg, Fraustadt, Oldenburg, Koblenz, and Karlsruhe. In 1903 he was appointed to be commanding general of the Fourth Army Corps in Magdeburg.

His was certainly a successful career for an officer in the army of the German Empire. But it was by no means an exceptional career. Hindenburg was never promoted because of unique achievements or outstanding performance. He did his duty and promptly carried out the orders he was given. He was granted the regular advances that came with seniority. Hindenburg was an adequate officer, not a brilliant one.

Yet in the culture of the German Empire, any officer, whether brilliant or not, enjoyed numerous privileges. Because Germany had been unified under Prussian leadership, the values associated with the Junkers, the leaders of Prussia, soon were recognized throughout the rest of society. Prussian officers were of noble birth, members of the time-honored aristocracy. Having been born into this class, they immediately garnered respect. The soldierly values of military honor and unquestioning obedience were widely held as virtues. Theodor Fontane, an important German novelist of the late 19th century, also describes the social results in many of his works, such as *Effi Briest*. A war correspondent during the Franco-Prussian War, Fontane was interested in realistically portraying the Prussian officers' lives amidst rapid social changes.

But a genuine historical event can best show how military values spread throughout all of German society. On October 18, 1906, an unemployed former convict, Wilhelm Vogt, bought a used officer's uniform in a secondhand store. Once he put it on, he looked like an officer, and he was treated like one. Previously his requests for employment papers and a residence permit had been turned down. In his new uniform, Vogt was able to take command of 10 soldiers in Berlin, travel to the suburb of Köpenick, and seize the city treasury. Although he was eventually arrested, he became a popular hero and received an imperial pardon. The kaiser was delighted with this proof of German respect for an army uniform.

In 1911, at the age of 64, Hindenburg retired from the army. After a successful, if undistinguished, career, he was not a well-known figure. He was just one more retired officer in the new German Empire. He settled near Hanover, spending his time hunting game and collecting art, especially paintings of Christian scenes, including the Madonna and Child — Mary and her son, Jesus. His two daughters had married Junkers, and his only son was now an officer in his former Third Regiment. Europe seemed to be at peace. The years would pass quietly, as they had after the Franco-Prussian War.

> *The consciousness of a special and personal relationship to the king, the loyalty of a vassal to his lord, permeated the whole life of an officer.*
> —PAUL VON HINDENBURG

3

A Hero by Luck

In the summer of 1914 Hindenburg was 66 years old. His long career in the military seemed to be over. Although it had not been extraordinarily eventful, it had been successful and had raised the Junker into the upper ranks of the German high command. General Hindenburg could settle into a peaceful retirement, while the German Empire, which had been declared at Versailles in 1871, seemed to be able to enjoy peace and relative prosperity.

Yet Hindenburg did not feel comfortable in his retirement. He had spent all his life as a soldier. Longingly, he recalled his years in active military service. Was there no place for him in the army anymore? Probably not. Europe was at peace, and another war did not seem likely.

However, there was great uneasiness among the European people. Like Hindenburg, dissatisfied with his retirement, many Europeans felt ill at ease with the political stability and their everyday routines. Since the turn of the century, a dissatisfaction had spread through the culture of Europe. There were those who believed that peace was temporary, even an illusion. They felt that Europe would soon erupt, sweeping aside the increasingly cumbersome traditions of the past, clearing the way for new scientific and social advances. The modern age would begin. The Russian revolutionary Vladimir Lenin, who in 1917 would help to establish a so-

For a soldier, war is the normal condition of affairs; and anyway, I am in God's hands.
—PAUL VON HINDENBURG

Hindenburg in 1897. After his promotion to the general staff the unexceptional officer rose methodically through the ranks and was stationed in various towns throughout Germany. He enjoyed the respect accorded army officers of the Junker class.

cialist government in Russia, called the approaching war "the great accelerator." Europe was on the verge of an explosion that would do away with the mighty kingdoms that had ruled the continent for centuries. Its cities were now noisy metropolises with massive populations. A large proportion of these populations shouldered the labor in Europe's factories. The sheer size of these masses was changing society. Both middle- and working-class people grew louder in their demands for a say in how their nations were governed.

Meanwhile, the European countries were caught in a web of political problems — the result mainly of many and complex alliances. They piled ever more powerful weapons along their shared frontiers. Great Britain, which had for centuries been the predominant naval power, now faced the challenge of a growing German fleet. Russia was anxious to expand its influence in the Balkan Peninsula in southeastern Europe. Russia's plans collided with the interests of the Austro-Hungarian Empire, with which the new German kaiser, Wilhelm II, had made an alliance. Peaceful Europe was a powder keg of modern weapons and secret treaties waiting to explode.

Suddenly, the first spark flew. Visiting the city of Sarajevo in the province of Bosnia (now part of Yugoslavia), the Austrian Archduke Franz Ferdinand was assassinated on June 28, 1914. With the support of the German Empire, the Austrian government protested and presented the Serbian government with strict demands. The Russians, who had formed a military alliance with France, backed tiny Serbia. Tensions in eastern Europe intensified, and the great armies of Austria-Hungary, Germany, and Russia were put on alert. Because France was an ally of Russia, and because of the long-standing hostility between France and Germany, the situation in western Europe became increasingly dangerous.

In the east, storm clouds of revolt had been gathering over Russia since 1905, when a revolution there had been suppressed by Tsar Nicholas II, the

The first panacea for a mismanaged nation is inflation of the currency; the second is war. Both bring a temporary prosperity; both bring a permanent ruin. But both are the refuge of political and economic opportunists.
—ERNEST HEMINGWAY
American author, in *Notes on the Next War*

38

nation's ruling monarch. Nevertheless, the tsar's armies were mobilized and readied for an attack on Germany on July 31, 1914. The next day, Germany declared war. World War I had begun. In August Russian armies invaded the German province of East Prussia, while Germany attacked France by marching through neutral Belgium. This violation of Belgian neutrality brought Great Britain into the war against Germany.

A wave of enthusiasm for the war had swept through Germany. Nearly all young men were more than willing to participate in the fighting. Crowds cheered for the soldiers on their way to fight the French and the Russians. The excitement over-shadowed all political disputes and any doubts about the wisdom of the war, which seemed fully justified. One lieutenant gave apt expression to the overall mood in August when he wrote that "war is like Christmas." On his way to the front, that same lieutenant died of an accidental gunshot wound. The optimism and idealism of August soon turned to disillusionment. Once the war was under way, another popular misconception — that the war would end quickly — would be shattered. The troops would not soon be marching home. France, Germany, Austria-Hungary, and Russia were locked in desperate combat. When the summer ended, the carnage of war went on.

The Germans saw that, though greatly outnumbered by the Russians, they possessed certain advantages over their adversary. One of these was geography. The terrain favored the Germans, because it was covered by numerous bodies of water, the so-called Masurian Lakes. In order to advance through the marshy lake region into German territory, the Russians would have to split their forces and thus lose the benefit of the tremendous size of their combined armies. In addition, the Germans could utilize their modern railway network on the German-held side of the lakes. Although their forces were smaller, their maneuverability was greater.

The Russian army, which was positioned north of the lakes, began to march due west on August

THE BETTMANN ARCHIVE

With imperial Germany's co-operation, Marxist revolutionary Vladimir Lenin was returned in 1917 from exile in Europe to Russia. He led the Bolshevik Revolution in the fall of that year, founding the Soviet Union. World War I, he said, was "the great accelerator."

EUROPE IN 1914

NORWAY

NORTH SEA

Stockholm

St. Petersburg

SWEDEN

BALTIC
SEA

GREAT BRITAIN

DENMARK

Copenhagen

Riga

RUSSIA

London

NETHERLANDS

Berlin

Warsaw

Brest Litovsk

BELGIUM

GERMANY

Brussels
LUX.

Paris

Cracow

ATLANTIC OCEAN

FRANCE

Zurich
SWITZ.

Vienna

Budapest

GALICIA

AUSTRIA-HUNGARY

ROMANIA

BOSNIA-
HERZ.

Bucharest

Sarajevo
Belgrade

PORTUGAL

Madrid

ITALY

MONTENEGRO

SERBIA

BULGARIA

Sofia

SPAIN

Rome

ALBANIA

GREECE

MEDITERRANEAN SEA

Athens

World War I (1914–18) changed the boundaries of Europe's nations and hastened the collapse of its tottering monarchies. When Austria-Hungary's Archduke Franz Ferdinand was assassinated by a Serbian nationalist, Austria declared war on tiny Serbia, causing the German Empire's immediate entry into the war.

17. Thus began the Battle of Gumbinnen. During the next few days, German counterattacks, led by General Hermann von François in violation of his commander's orders, inflicted serious damage on the Russians. Nevertheless, Rennenkampf, the Russian general, was not defeated, but only slowed down. On the evening of August 20, the German commander, Lieutenant General Max von Prittwitz, learned that the Russian Second Army, under General Aleksandr Samsonov, was now also advancing, from the south, toward the lake region.

Prittwitz panicked. Afraid that the two Russian armies would surround him, he told his officers to order all units to retreat. This meant falling back to behind the Vistula River inside East Prussia. He sent a telegram to the German general headquarters in Koblenz, warning that the advancing Russian armies could be stopped only with the help of reinforcements from the west.

To Lieutenant Colonel Max von Hoffmann, the deputy chief of operations, fighting the Russians was not a matter for "weak characters." Despite his low opinion of Prittwitz, Hoffmann explained to him why a retreat was unnecessary and how the Russian invasion could be blocked. Prittwitz took Hoffmann's advice and seemed to regain his confidence. But he forgot to inform the headquarters in Koblenz of the sudden change in plans.

Because of this oversight, the German commander in chief, Field Marshal Helmuth von Moltke, was left with the impression that the eastern line of defense had collapsed. Moltke decided to take two steps to remedy the crisis. First, he ordered that reinforcements be sent to the east. Second, he ordered that Prittwitz be relieved of his command of the Eighth Army.

Hindenburg and Ludendorff arrived at the eastern headquarters on the evening of August 24. Hoffmann's point of view had prevailed. Plans for a retreat were abandoned. Instead, a German offensive would soon be under way. Hindenburg and Ludendorff had arrived to take charge of this new strategy.

During the next two days, most of the German forces were moved toward the Russian army in the south. Only a thin defensive line in the north faced Rennenkampf, who was still recovering from a bruising encounter with the Germans. The plan was to defeat Samsonov in the south while hiding from Rennenkampf the weakness in the German lines in the north. It was a strategic gamble, for if Rennenkampf were to decide to advance, the Germans would be trapped between the two armies.

But Hindenburg was lucky. Thanks to captured documents, he knew that Russian communications and supply lines had become extremely inefficient. The Germans, however, were greatly aided by their efficient railway system. For example, it was by railroad that troops, led by the aggressive, often disobedient General François, were transported to their positions for the next major clash. Hindenburg also benefited from the fact that the two Russian armies communicated with each other by radio

Kaiser Wilhelm II of Germany and Emperor Franz Josef of Austria, who had ruled his nation for 66 years by 1914. While Tsar Nicholas II of Russia pledged to fight on France's side in the event of war, Wilhelm ignored his cabinet's advice and guaranteed Franz Josef unconditional military support.

messages that were often not transmitted in code. Even when they were in code, the Russian codes were not difficult to crack, so the German forces were always aware of their enemy's next move.

Possibly Hindenburg's greatest stroke of luck had to do with the relationship between the two Russian generals. Hoffmann explained before the battle that a decade earlier, during the Russo-Japanese War (1904—05), Rennenkampf and Samsonov had quarreled and engaged in a brawl. Rennenkampf had failed to assist Samsonov in a battle against the Japanese the Russians might otherwise have won. They continued the feud, and Hoffmann was certain that if Samsonov came under attack, Rennenkampf would not come to the rescue of his old rival.

Gavrilo Princip of Serbia (now part of Yugoslavia) is dragged off to prison after assassinating Austrian Archduke Franz Ferdinand and his wife, Duchess Sophie, in Sarajevo. Russian troops were mobilized days after war was declared on Serbia; the Russian army soon marched into East Prussia, and Hindenburg's military career started anew.

Whether true or not, events seemed to confirm Hoffmann's theory.

The Battle of Tannenberg began on August 26, 1914. Named for a small village in East Prussia (now Stebark, Poland), the battle sprawled along an area ranging more than 60 miles. To the Germans, this confrontation with the Russians was crucial for more than one reason. Clearly, it would help determine the course of military events in the east. Whichever nation won the battle would very likely win the war in the region. But Tannenberg also represented a significant past event to the Germans. It seemed as important psychologically as militarily for Hindenburg to achieve a victory here. Centuries earlier, in the 1200s, the Teutonic Knights had established their own society in Prussia, known as the "Order." They had served in the Third Crusade (1189–92), one of a series of wars launched by Christian Europe against Muslim forces in the Middle East and the Mediterranean. These knights soon gained both financial and military strength in eastern Europe. Their territorial control spread as far as the Balkans to the south. Then, in 1410 the Polish king, Ladislas II, challenged the knights with an army of Poles, Bohemians, Lithuanians, and Russians. In the resulting battle at Tannenberg, the knights and their empire were dealt a crushing defeat. Now, more than 500 years later, the Germans hoped for a different outcome.

By presenting a weak center line, the German army tempted Samsonov to move forward, while German forces advanced on the right and left flanks. By evening, the Germans were beginning to encircle the Russian army. Samsonov attempted to retreat to the east, but he could not break through the German lines. He even appealed to Rennenkampf for help from the north, but the old feud proved stronger than the need to defeat the Germans. Rennenkampf stood by idly while the German army under Hindenburg's command overpowered the Russian forces in the south.

By August 30, when the battle ended, more than 100,000 Russian soldiers had been killed and an

Remember, if Tannenberg had not gone well for us, there would have been a name cursed by all Germans through eternity: the name of Hindenburg.
—PAUL VON HINDENBURG

equal number taken prisoner. In a forest near where the battle was fought, the Germans found Samsonov's body. The evidence indicated that he had committed suicide, possibly to escape dishonor for the defeat or to avoid the indignity of being captured by the Germans.

If Rennenkampf had attacked the Germans immediately, his fresh troops might have succeeded in achieving victory. But he waited more than a week, giving Hindenburg the time to reorganize his forces. Although Hindenburg was said to have had an ancestor who fought in the 15th-century battle, it was not his idea to name the 20th-century German victory after Tannenberg. Ludendorff claimed credit for the notion, but probably it was that of Lieutenant Colonel Hoffmann, the German general staff's expert on Russian affairs.

After Samsonov's Second Army was virtually destroyed at Tannenberg, Hindenburg ordered the Eighth Army to maneuver to face Rennenkampf's First Army. In the meantime, as earlier requested by Prittwitz, troops that had been fighting against France had been brought to Russia to help Hindenburg's army at Tannenberg. Because the battle was already won these reinforcements were no longer necessary; however, they were badly needed against the French. It is often said that the decision to move two army corps to the east later cost Germany the famed Battle of the Marne in France, which was fought from August 20 until August 24. There, French General Joffre stopped the Germans' march on Paris. Concerning this issue, British historian A. J. P. Taylor writes, "Of course, Germany would have had more forces available for the western front if the Franco-Russian alliance had not existed; but in that case France and Germany would not have been at war."

On September 5 the First Battle of the Masurian Lakes began. (A second battle would be fought in the area in the winter of 1915.) It lasted until September 18. When the German attack began, Rennenkampf retreated. To guard against the bold General Francois's lightning-fast move to encircle

him, he threw his forces against Ludendorff's troops in the center. This served to delay the Germans' advance, but the Russians were soon driven from East Prussia. Rennenkampf, who supposedly abandoned his troops to defeat, was dismissed by the tsar.

Tannenberg and the First Battle of the Masurian Lakes were among the first significant German victories of World War I. The Russians, despite their superior numbers, had been defeated, and the name of the German commander, previously unknown, became internationally famous. Hindenburg was immediately turned into a national hero with the help of clever propaganda and his own ancestral

German commander in chief, Field Marshal Helmuth Johannes von Moltke, seen with Kaiser Wilhelm II (left), was replaced by General Erich von Falkenhayn, who in turn was replaced by Hindenburg as the German army's supreme commander. Moltke had sent reinforcements to fight in Russia when these troops were badly needed against the French.

45

General Aleksandr Samsonov commanded the Russian Second Army. His forces and General Pavel Rennenkampf's First Army comprised the Russian "steamroller," expected to flatten the German army. Left isolated by Rennenkampf, Samsonov's army was trapped and wiped out by Hindenburg and Ludendorff at Tannenberg.

past. He became a symbol of the German nation at war. But the hero had been very lucky. His success was due less to his own military skill than to other factors, such as Prittwitz's confusion, Hoffmann's intelligence, easy access to Russian battle plans, the superior German railroad system, and the apparent feud between the Russian generals. Also, had François obeyed orders rather than rushing ahead, the outcome might have been different.

Perhaps Hindenburg's largest contribution was steadying Ludendorff's nerves — the "inward crisis," Hindenburg had called it. Nevertheless, Hindenburg was a hero to a nation searching for heroic leaders. He was flooded with mail from admirers throughout Germany. Streets, squares, and restaurants were named after him. Soon giant wooden statues of the hero of Tannenberg were erected in many German cities. Nails were sold (the proceeds went to the German Red Cross), which purchasers were allowed to hammer into these statues. Hindenburg represented an image of Germany sworn to defeat the enemy.

As the war dragged on, the kaiser tended to withdraw from public view. Meanwhile, the German chancellor, Theobald von Bethmann Hollweg, was unable to captivate the public. Hindenburg, instead, became Germany's leading figure. He personified strength, authority, and German national feeling.

Hindenburg personally encouraged this adulation. His statements to the press were phrased to fit his new image. In addition, he was constantly accompanied by a painter, Hugo Vogel. The artist was expected always to portray Hindenburg as a towering hero and a reassuring leader.

The battles in East Prussia could be used to transform Hindenburg into such a compelling symbol for the Germans because these victories contrasted so sharply with the course of the war elsewhere. German soldiers had fought valiantly on the western front, of course. Yet nowhere could a German commander point to a campaign as successful and decisive as Hindenburg's defeat of the invading Russians in August and September 1914. The feared Russian "steamroller," despite its vast size, had been pushed back by superior planning and leadership.

The fundamental German strategy against France in World War I had been sketched in advance and was called the Schlieffen Plan. General Alfred von Schlieffen, who developed the plan, was regarded by the Germans as their supreme military strategist. His doctrines were studied by every Prussian officer. He believed that victory in a European war depended above all on a victory over the other major continental military power, France. Schlieffen argued

Maps show the strategy that led to Hindenburg's triumph at Tannenberg against the armies of Generals Samsonov and Rennenkampf. Hindenburg and Ludendorff's offensive against the Russians here was aided by the Prussian railway, uncoded Russian messages, and the bitter rivalry between the two Russian commanders.

THE BATTLE OF TANNENBERG

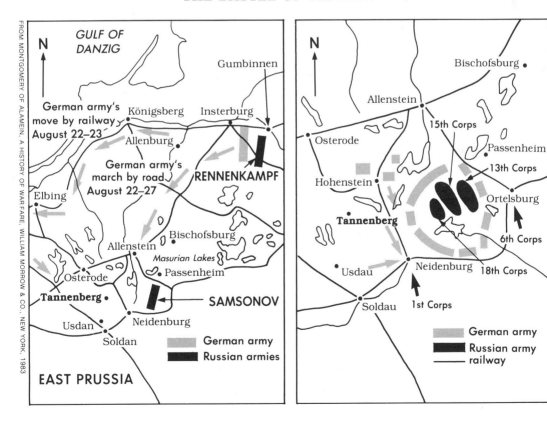

that in order to defeat France, Germany would have to attack through northern France and advance toward Paris and the coast so as to block any assistance from Britain. This plan was also referred to as the "swinging door," since these two armies would essentially pivot around a "hinge" like a closing door. As the French armies were enveloped, they would be cut off from outside help at the same time.

Because the invasion of France was considered all-important, most of Germany's troops and supplies were deployed accordingly. Schlieffen stated that Germany should not place too many troops either in Alsace and Lorraine (provinces taken from France in 1871) or in the east against Russia. It would be better, according to the Schlieffen Plan, to retreat in the south and the east, as long as the invasion in the northern area of the western front succeeded, for it was in the north that victory would be decided.

When the war began in August, the German commander began by repeatedly ignoring the Schlieffen Plan. Troops were sent from the west to the panic-stricken Prittwitz in the east, and troops from the north bolstered the defense in the south. The result was catastrophic for German war objectives. After a quick advance into France and Belgium, which provoked the British to enter the war, the German invasion came to a halt. The German march toward Paris failed.

Because of the collapse of the Schlieffen Plan and the unsuccessful Battle of the Marne, Moltke, the chief of the general staff, was replaced by General Erich von Falkenhayn, a former Prussian minister of war. This change took place on September 14, 1914, but was not made public until November. In fact, the grave situation on the western front was covered up in statements made by government officials. Public attention was directed instead to the events in East Prussia. The successes in the battles of Tannenberg and the Masurian Lakes were less important than the failures in France. Yet Hindenburg was increasingly the subject of legend and hero worship, while the public was kept in the dark concerning how serious the military situation was in the west.

In November 1914 Hindenburg was promoted to the rank of field marshal. As the forces under Hindenburg racked up victories against the Russians, his reputation grew. Hindenburg's victories contrasted sharply with the prolonged inability of Falkenhayn to achieve a victory in the west, where German casualties in Belgium and France had been severe.

In February 1915 a second battle took place in the Masurian Lakes region. Aiming to destroy the enemy's fighting capabilities, Hindenburg and Ludendorff ordered the German Eighth Army to advance against the Russians. They attacked during a blizzard. Stunned, the Russians began retreating and were nearly trapped when Hindenburg swung his newly formed Tenth Army at them from the north. Though the extreme cold had been an obstacle for the Germans, they won the battle and inflicted heavy casualties on the Russians.

A competition developed between Falkenhayn and Hindenburg, the two highest-ranking German military leaders. Deprived of any good opportunity for victory in the west, Falkenhayn decided to direct a new campaign in the east. After General August von Mackensen had demolished the Russian Third Army, the Germans then stormed through the gap that had been cleared between the Polish towns of Gorlice and Tarnów. With the Russians scattered by the onslaught, the Germans were free to march on Warsaw and Brest Litovsk. Falkenhayn, who soon returned to the west, had taken charge of the attack on these two cities and the Russian defeat at Gorlice-Tarnów. Reflecting well on Falkenhayn, these victories bolstered German confidence and humiliated the Russians. The Russian commander in chief, Grand Duke Nikolai Nikolaevich, saw his colossal army forced to retreat. It was on the run and on the defensive. Poorly supplied, with shortages of both food and ammunition, the grand duke was helpless to lead hungry, barely trained recruits against this better-equipped, more efficient enemy. Tsar Nicholas II took personal control of the Russian army in 1915. As a result, Russia's position did not improve; the tsar's command led only to further disasters. Casualties, by this time, were huge: Rus-

> *I admit this was a mistake, for which retribution came on the Marne.*
> —FIELD MARSHAL VON MOLTKE on the decision to move two German army corps to the eastern front

UPI/BETTMANN NEWSPHOTOS

Generals Hindenburg (left) and Ludendorff (right) flank Kaiser Wilhelm II. In February 1915, when the Russians met defeat in the Second Battle of the Masurian Lakes, Wilhelm declared, "The enemy must be utterly destroyed. Then I will dictate the peace terms at the points of my soldiers' bayonets."

sians killed, wounded, and taken prisoner totaled approximately 3 million.

Because of his mass popularity, Hindenburg now had many supporters in political circles. In addition, Falkenhayn was opposed by others, among them Theobald Bethmann Hollweg, the German chancellor, who disliked Falkenhayn's insistence on a major victory in the west. Some recognized that such a victory had become impossible and that Germany ought to attempt a negotiated settlement to put an end to the war.

On the western front, Falkenhayn's efforts to seize the fortress of Verdun had met with no success, but the toll in lives was enormous. Falkenhayn had intended the offensive at Verdun to be a knockout blow against the French. French and British troops were attacking German lines along the Somme River. In the east, a Russian advance was able to push aside the Fourth and Seventh Austrian Armies and take 25,000 prisoners. Hindenburg, now with fewer troops, commanded the defensive line along

Tsar Nicholas II, on horseback, holds a Russian religious icon as soldiers swear allegiance to him. Nicholas took personal command of the Russian army in 1915 after the previous year's defeats at Tannenberg and the Masurian Lakes — important victories for both Hindenburg and Ludendorff.

the eastern front against General Alexei Brusilov. Falkenhayn was further discredited when Germany was put on the defensive everywhere, while her allies were collapsing. Romania entered the war against Germany, bringing an army of three-quarters of a million new troops.

After devoting much thought to the problem and listening to many arguments, the kaiser was finally persuaded to remove Falkenhayn and appoint Hindenburg as chief of the general staff of the entire German army on August 29, 1916, two years after the German victory at Tannenberg. Ludendorff was made quartermaster general, formally second in command of the general staff, but in fact he was to share command with Hindenburg.

Chancellor Bethmann Hollweg was Germany's highest-ranking political official aside from the kaiser himself. He hoped that the removal of Falkenhayn would increase the chances for negotiating peace. But the appointment of Hindenburg had an enormous impact on the way important decisions

Chief of staff Hindenburg (left) and Quartermaster General Ludendorff in 1916. That year, General Falkenhayn, who favored concentrating on the war against the French and British rather than against the Russians, was removed as chief of staff by the kaiser.

were made in Germany during the war. Hindenburg was becoming a living legend whose massive popularity was eclipsing both the kaiser and chancellor. A naval battle cruiser was named the *Hindenburg* in honor of the chief of staff. In his new position, Hindenburg saw fit to establish an *Oberste Kriegsleitung*, or Supreme War Command, in September. Hindenburg thus also became personally responsible for leading the armies of Austria-Hungary, Bulgaria, and Turkey.

The kaiser became less and less interested in taking an active role in making decisions as the war continued. He increasingly inspired criticism rather than praise, since not all Germans were pleased with the war or with the widespread hunger and pain it caused. Many aristocrats, as well as economically hard-hit workers, began to lose confidence in Wilhelm II. A vacuum of power had begun to form in the German government. Meanwhile, followers of the radical socialist agitator Rosa Luxemburg had taken to the streets and demanded an end to the war. She was joined by a former member of the German Social Democratic party, Karl Liebknecht, who had been the lone defender of her antiwar position in the *Reichstag* (Parliament). Germany's workmen had nothing to gain from the war, Luxemburg and Liebknecht argued, and instead should overthrow the government. The two radicals became the leaders of the "Spartacist" movement. Liebknecht had begun openly agitating against the war in 1916 and was briefly imprisoned. The author of several pamphlets urging German workers to revolt, Liebknecht signed these writings "Spartacus," after the 1st-century B.C. Roman gladiator and rebel.

After August, when Ludendorff was named co-commander of the German armed forces, he and Hindenburg seemed to become indispensable to the kaiser's government. Just as he had planned much of the Battle of Tannenberg with Hindenburg's approval, Ludendorff would continue to initiate policy. Whenever there was a difference of opinion with the chancellor, Ludendorff would refuse to be held responsible for the chancellor's ideas or for their possible consequences. As a result, Ludendorff almost always got his way. Also, since the outbreak of the war, Germany's various political parties had agreed to call off their usual competition. Moreover, they had agreed to give the government their support for the duration of the war. This agreement was referred to as the *Burgfrieden.*

I decline Christianity because it is Jewish, because it is international, and because, in cowardly fashion, it preaches the doctrine of Peace on Earth.
—ERICH VON LUDENDORFF
German military leader

4

Peace Stalks the Warrior

By the summer of 1916, the war was going very poorly for Germany. This dire situation confronted Hindenburg after he took over the Supreme Command at the end of August. Chancellor Bethmann Hollweg had helped engineer the removal of Falkenhayn and the appointment of Hindenburg. Bethmann Hollweg hoped that Hindenburg, with his maturity, experience, and popular appeal, would be able to prevent the war from dragging on. He believed that a negotiated peace remained possible.

The United States was still neutral, and the American president, Woodrow Wilson, was eager to mediate between the warring parties. If Germany was to seize the opportunity Wilson offered, Hindenburg would have to provide the political leadership. But Hindenburg was not a politician. He was a Junker and a soldier. He had a chance to sue for peace, but he used his power to continue the war. His sense of duty forced him to try to win the war at any cost, and this compulsion blinded him to the increasing likelihood of a German defeat.

As the German situation in the war became more dangerous, Hindenburg became politically more powerful. He controlled the German army and the

Repeatedly in the course of the war, we could have had a peace by agreement, if it had not been that the boundless demands of the German militaristic-conservative combine made it impossible. It is fearful and tragic that this combine could be broken only by the overthrow of the whole state.
—FRIEDRICH MEINECKE
German historian

Field Marshal Hindenburg (right) with General Hans von Seeckt during World War I. Hindenburg's popularity in Germany never waned, and in 1916 he became chief of the general staff after Falkenhayn failed to defeat the French at Verdun.

forces of the German allies as well: Austria-Hungary, Turkey, and Bulgaria. Six million troops were under his command, and he could exercise enormous control over domestic politics and the German economy. Nevertheless, his background as a Junker and his training in the Prussian army had taught him to disdain politics.

Hindenburg's dislike for politics and diplomacy and his commitment to military duty became clear immediately after his appointment at the end of August. As soon as he had been appointed to replace his former rival, Falkenhayn, he adopted the same point of view that Falkenhayn had presented: a stunning German victory in the west was the only way to end the war. Yet the French were receiving aid from the British, and both were increasingly dependent on American supplies. The German economy, meanwhile, was suffering from shortages. The German army would be able to gain the upper hand in the west only if the enemy's transatlantic supply lines were cut.

Although the German fleet of battleships had been greatly expanded before the war, it was unable to match the British navy. The Germans had one remaining option: unrestricted submarine warfare. This also was the answer to the problem of blocking the Allied supply line. Unrestricted submarine warfare meant sinking any foreign ships bringing supplies to the Allies, whether they belonged to the

A float publicizing relief efforts for war-ravaged France parades down a New York street. Prior to sending troops to Europe in 1917 to help the British and French defeat the kaiser's army, the United States sent food (and covert military assistance) to its future allies.

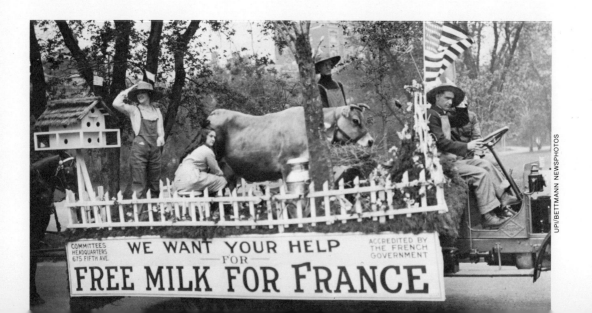

COMMITTEES
HEADQUARTERS
675 FIFTH AVE.
WE WANT YOUR HELP
—FOR—
ACCREDITED BY
THE FRENCH
GOVERNMENT
FREE MILK FOR FRANCE

enemy or to neutral powers — such as the United States. It meant sinking all foreign ships, civilian or military.

The Germans had already shown their willingness to use terror against civilian populations. Such tactics were designed to hurt the enemy by destroying morale as well as material and human resources. When the Germans invaded Belgium, they earned a reputation as barbarian "Huns" by shooting civilians and burning farms and towns. They sacked and put to the torch the city of Louvain, including its famed library, built in the 15th century. Meant by the Germans to instill fear and respect, these actions only further infuriated the Allies. At sea, German use of submarines against world shipping brought the United States into the war to help defeat the kaiser's forces. On May 7, 1915, a German submarine sank the British ocean liner *Lusitania*. Of the 1,959 passengers and crew aboard, 1,198 drowned, including 128 U.S. citizens. The United States had already issued a protest against the German submarine policy. It stated that the sinking of U.S. ships or killing of U.S. citizens by Germany would be considered "an indefensible violation of neutral rights." Though unarmed, the *Lusitania*, it was found, was carrying a shipment of rifles and ammunition. If another such incident occurred, the United States was sure to join the war against Germany.

On January 9, 1917, a meeting took place at Pless Castle. The kaiser was present, as were Hindenburg, Ludendorff, Chancellor Bethmann Hollweg,

Captured German submarines, or U-boats. In 1915 a German submarine sank the ocean liner *Lusitania*, killing 1,198 civilians. Unrestricted submarine warfare was intended to terrify the enemy and wreak havoc on neutral and Allied shipping. Hindenburg defended this policy that helped bring the United States into the war.

and other military and governmental leaders. The chancellor hoped to prevent an adoption of unrestricted submarine warfare because he feared the entry of the United States into the war. But the representatives of the military insisted that the use of submarines would stop the flow of supplies across the Atlantic. Admiral von Holtzendorf, the chief of the naval staff, even assured the kaiser that the United States was of no concern, saying, "I give Your Majesty my word as an officer that not one American will land on the continent."

Hindenburg was not as certain as Holtzendorf concerning war with the United States. But in agreement with Ludendorff, he argued for continuing the submarine campaign. Hindenburg and the military were able to convince the kaiser, and a policy of unrestricted submarine warfare was adopted. Bethmann Hollweg had correctly predicted the result. The freedom of the seas and the rights of neutral powers, including the United States, were seen as under attack. Efforts by the United States to find a nonmilitary answer to the war in Europe came to an end. On February 3, 1917, diplomatic relations ceased between the United States and Germany, and on April 6 the United States declared war on that country. At about this time 881,000 tons of shipping were sent to the bottom by German submarines. By November, American troops were fighting alongside their French and British allies. Hindenburg and the German military leaders had sacrificed political foresight to the goal of stopping the flow of enemy supplies. But they had miscalculated on this point as well, for the submarines could not prevent munitions or more than 2 million U.S. troops from arriving in Europe.

The adoption of submarine warfare was a fatal blow to the influence of Chancellor Bethmann Hollweg. By the middle of the summer, the Supreme Command (Hindenburg and Ludendorff) succeeded in having him removed from office. Faced with the threat of either resignation by both Hindenburg and Ludendorff or dismissing Bethmann Hollweg, the kaiser preferred the latter. The Reichstag helped to unseat Bethman Hollweg, and power was trans-

The blast of the hand-grenades impinges powerfully on our arms and legs; crouching like cats we run on, overwhelmed by this wave that bears us along, that fills us with ferocity, turns us into thugs, into murderers, into God knows what devils. . . . If your own father came over with [the enemy] you would not hesitate to fling a bomb at him.
—ERICH MARIA REMARQUE
German novelist, in *All Quiet on the Western Front*

ferred to the military. His successor, Georg Michaelis, was an unknown bureaucrat who was able to serve as the mouthpiece of the military. The weak democratic structures in the parliamentary monarchy of the German Empire dissolved. By the end of 1917 Hindenburg and Ludendorff's military dictatorship had been made complete.

Hindenburg had always distrusted politicians and had resented the fact that the chancellor, Bethmann Hollweg, had attempted to decide military affairs. It seemed to him that politicians and legislatures always interfered with the genuine exercise of power. His training in the Cadet Corps and the elitism of the German officer corps to which he belonged caused Hindenburg to approve of forceful, uncompromising leadership during a crisis. Yet this kind of leadership, which won the debate over submarine warfare, ended up pushing the United States into the war against Germany. This military regime showed that it was not skilled in negotiations when Germany and Russia later discussed arrangements for peace.

In March 1917 a revolution had forced Tsar Nicholas II to abdicate the Russian throne. After the tsar's fall, the provisional government that took power was overthrown in November (October, according to the Russian old calendar) by the Bolsheviks, or Russian communists, led by Vladimir Lenin. Germany had allowed Lenin to cross its territory by train on his way back to Russia from exile. The Bolsheviks had long opposed continuing the war with Germany, and an armistice was signed in December. Peace negotiations with the Germans were carried out at Brest Litovsk, Poland, by Leon Trotsky, an important Bolshevik revolutionary acting as envoy. At Brest Litovsk, the German government failed to show the world that they could deal generously with those whom they had defeated. The German leadership presented their grand plans to annex parts of Russia. A harsh treaty was imposed on the Russians and signed on March 3, 1918. The Germans claimed 301,000 square miles of Russian territory. Thus the Treaty of Brest Litovsk undermined the position of moderates in the Allied countries who

UPI/BETTMANN NEWSPHOTOS

Soviet delegates arrive in Brest Litovsk in 1918 to conduct peace negotiations with the Germans, who had overwhelmed the Russians in World War I. Talks began in December 1917, after Lenin's Bolsheviks had seized power in Russia. Chief Soviet delegate Leon Trotsky found the Germans determined to annex Russian territory.

When Germany persisted in waging unrestricted submarine warfare in 1916, ignoring U.S. protests that the policy was "an indefensible violation of neutral rights," President Woodrow Wilson asked Congress to declare war on Germany on April 2, 1917. Months earlier, Hindenburg, agreeing with Ludendorff, told the kaiser: "The submarine campaign must go ahead."

had believed it was worthwhile to attempt reaching a peaceful settlement with the Germans. Instead, the Germans' huge appetite for conquest frightened many away from anything but a policy of defeating Germany.

Not only did the Treaty of Brest Litovsk harm Germany's diplomatic standing, but it also weakened it militarily. For in order to enforce the treaty, Hindenburg had to leave a large army of occupation in the east, even though these troops were desperately needed on the western front.

Yet Hindenburg and the military leadership were committed to the policy of German expansion; the Treaty of Brest Litovsk gave ample proof of this. To annex territory in the east as well as Belgium and parts of northern France was deemed necessary to protect the nation from foreign and domestic enemies. The leadership feared that, given the expectations of the German people, a social revolution might break out in Germany if the war ended without major territorial gains. Naturally, Hindenburg fully supported annexation. In November 1917 Michaelis was replaced by Count Georg von Hertling. Meanwhile, the secretary of state for foreign affairs, Richard von Kühlmann, attempted to curb Ludendorff's power. He, too, was dismissed, both for not being aggressive enough in the treaty negotiations with the Russians and for suggesting that Germany could not win the war. In fact, the desperation with which the war was pursued, beginning in 1916, was due to the likelihood that a defeat of the German army would reduce the prestige and power of the military and the Junkers in Germany after the war. If the imperial army did not win, the empire itself might crumble.

Signs of unrest were beginning to appear in Germany. Shortages began to affect the home population. Disappointing news from the fronts fueled opposition to the war. Although Hindenburg and the Supreme Command declared strikes illegal, a major strike broke out in January 1918. In Berlin alone, half a million workers walked off their jobs, protesting the war and its economic effects. The military responded by declaring a state of siege. Workers who were in the army reserve were called to duty, and seven major industrial firms were placed under martial law.

As political choices dwindled, Hindenburg decided in favor of the military solution. On March 21 he launched a general offensive in northern France toward the railway center at Amiens. The Germans managed to break through the British lines, but since so many troops were kept pinned down in the east, reinforcements were unavailable to make the drive a success. While the offensive was still in progress, the kaiser hailed the operation as the greatest ever in history. He awarded Hindenburg a medal that had been issued to only one general before him — Gebhard von Blücher, for helping to defeat Napoleon at Waterloo.

The offensive petered out by April 4. Hindenburg tried again that month and in May, but these new offensives were no more successful. By the middle of the summer of 1918 the military advantage had clearly passed to the other side. The British and French were aided now by 2 million fresh American troops, who had arrived in Europe despite Holtzendorf's previous assurances to the kaiser. On August 8, east of Amiens, British troops attacked, and for the first time the German army began to collapse. Though still unwilling to admit defeat, the Germans now stood no chance of winning.

United States Army recruits leave New York Armory following enlistment in 1917. After 881,000 tons of shipping were sunk by German submarines, German Chancellor Theobald von Bethmann Hollweg's fear that the United States would enter the war against Germany came true on April 6. Unable to control Hindenburg and Ludendorff's influence, Bethmann Hollweg resigned.

5
Defeat and Revolution

For one last time, Hindenburg launched an attack, but the German offensives during the spring and summer of 1918 failed. The costs of this desperate strategy were staggering. The turning point came on August 8. The British army was able to break through the German lines at Amiens. Ludendorff, who had consistently argued for continuing the war, later said that this single day in August "put the decline of our fighting power beyond all doubt." For the next three months, the Germans gradually retreated before the advancing Allies, aided by fresh American troops.

The Germans fought on, but the morale of the soldiers was rapidly weakening. At Amiens, for the first time, entire German divisions allowed themselves to be captured without offering any resistance. They had realized that their situation was hopeless.

The same pessimism began to spread through the military leadership. Even Ludendorff began to accept the impossibility of a German victory. Yet Hindenburg, convinced by now of his own myth of invulnerability, remained unworried. How could the hero of Tannenberg lead the armies of the German Empire to defeat? Hindenburg could not understand the situation's urgency, since Ludendorff and his staff had shielded him from the news of recent developments.

The main enemy is at home.
—KARL LIEBKNECHT
German socialist politician,
at the outbreak of
World War I

War Invalids Playing Cards by the artist Otto Dix, whose work from the early 1920s reflects the influence of his contemporary George Grosz and his own experience as a German soldier taken prisoner by the French. Art and literature in post-World War I Germany expressed the war's brutal intensity and the ensuing economic and political chaos.

UPI/BETTMANN NEWSPHOTOS

German troops captured in Belgium in 1918. The Germans' official policy of terror in Belgium early in World War I earned them a reputation as barbarian "Huns." By the spring of 1918 Germany was exhausted, its population desperate to see the war end. But Hindenburg launched another offensive.

The soldier and the army, not parliamentary majorities and decisions, have welded the German Empire together. I put my trust in the army.

—KAISER WILHELM II

On August 14 Kaiser Wilhelm met with the Supreme Command and high political officials to discuss the significance of the recent losses. The meeting took place at the German general headquarters in the town of Spa, a small Belgian resort. It was the last chance for the military to admit the impossibility of a German victory and the urgency of pursuing a negotiated settlement.

Tragically, none of the representatives of the German army were willing to confess their failure to their emperor. They concealed the fact that the British victory at Amiens on August 8 was the beginning of the end. They suggested to the kaiser that the German army would be able to hold on to territorial gains. They repeated claims that Germany would be able to win the war.

The kaiser believed Hindenburg, and the results were disastrous. The kaiser and the officials of the government were left with the impression that the circumstances were not critical. There was no reason to rush into peace negotiations, for they had been led to believe that the longer they waited the better Germany's position would become. But the opposite was true. The German leadership deceived itself and the nation. On August 21 the chancellor told the Reichstag in Berlin that "there is no ground for doubting our victory."

Even as late as August 1918 Hindenburg's prestige and the power of the myth of Tannenberg kept hidden the reality of the coming defeat. During Sep-

64

tember the situation continued to worsen. On September 2 the German lines were broken near Cambrai, and 10 days later the French scored another major victory. On September 15, Bulgaria, one of Germany's allies, ceased fighting; Turkey, another ally, was thoroughly defeated by the British in the Middle East. Austria-Hungary was preparing to make a separate peace. Germany was isolated as enemy forces approached the borders, and at home a weary public was calling for an end to the war.

On September 28 Ludendorff told Hindenburg what he had known for at least six weeks — a German victory was impossible. Defeat was coming soon, and peace negotiations were urgently needed. Hindenburg listened silently. His own illusions of victory finally vanished. As he had constantly done throughout his four-year cooperation with Ludendorff, he agreed and consented to the other man's plans.

The next morning, Hindenburg and Ludendorff met with the kaiser at his residence in Spa. They explained the military situation to him. If the war did not end quickly, they argued, Germany was certain to be defeated, and the kaiser's rule was likely to be abolished. In order to rapidly halt the fighting and also preserve the tradition of the imperial dynasty, Hindenburg and Ludendorff urged the kaiser to rally his people around him by establishing a parliamentary government and promising a new constitution. Kaiser Wilhelm agreed to this plan of Ludendorff's to carry out "a revolution from above," hoping to prevent a revolution from below. But it was too late, and the military leadership would once again fail to understand political conditions in Germany.

On October 3 Hindenburg sent a letter to the new German chancellor, Prince Max of Baden, stating that an immediate armistice was necessary. He wrote, "Owing to the breakdown on the Macedonian front, whereby a weakening of our reserves is necessitated, and in consequence of the impossibility of making good our very heavy losses in the battles of the last few days, there no longer exists any prospect, according to human calculation, of forcing

Kaiser Wilhelm II and his wife in exile at Doorn Castle, Holland. At first in favor of ending the war in October 1918, Hindenburg instead ordered another offensive. The new campaign ignited radical uprisings in many German cities, and in November Hindenburg urged the kaiser to flee to Holland for his own safety.

In November 1918 the city of Berlin was paralyzed by a general strike. The demonstrators, led by the Spartacist Karl Liebknecht, were trying to force an end to the war and install a revolutionary socialist government in Berlin.

peace upon our enemies. . . . In these circumstances it is imperative to stop fighting in order to spare the German people and its allies further useless sacrifices." This is an important document because it marks Hindenburg's realization that the German army could not win.

The new chancellor had been initially reluctant to reach an immediate peace, but Hindenburg's letter convinced him that the circumstances were urgent. Unlike Ludendorff, the prince looked favorably upon the Fourteen Points, Wilson's peace proposal. Originally introduced before the United States Congress in January 1918, Wilson's plan stated the need to settle the war openly and fairly. Among its specific requirements were "absolute freedom" of the seas, restoration of Alsace-Lorraine to France, an independent Polish nation, and an "adjustment" of claims to colonies. Its last point stated the need for a "general association" of nations — the League of Nations. Early in the morning of October 4 a telegram calling for an armistice was sent to President Wilson, who replied in a polite manner, and negotiations began.

Suddenly Hindenburg's earlier support for unrestricted submarine warfare came back to haunt him. On October 12, in the midst of the negotiations for the armistice that Germany so direly needed, a German submarine torpedoed the passenger boat *Leinster*, which had sailed from Dublin. Nearly 200 British and American passengers died, and for weeks their bodies were swept onto the coasts of England and Ireland.

The *Leinster* incident enraged the public in the United States, and President Wilson toughened his stance. Earlier he had promised not to interfere in Germany's internal affairs. In his note of October 14, however, two days after the tragedy, he insisted that the kaiser give up his throne. Wilson would not support a peace agreement unless the Germans had a democracy.

Like many others, Wilson believed that Germany's long history of nondemocratic forms of government

Government troops battle Spartacist revolutionaries in Berlin. The Social Democrat leader Friedrich Ebert faced a huge challenge when he became chancellor in November 1918, beset by leftist uprisings at home and general defeat on the battlefront.

American Red Cross workers and sailors of the U.S. Navy with British soldiers celebrate German acceptance of the armistice on November 11, 1918, representing Allied victory over the shattered German Empire. Assured by Ebert's new government that it would combat leftist revolutionaries, Hindenburg returned the army peacefully to Germany.

had fostered militarism. Therefore, he called for "the destruction of every arbitrary power anywhere that can separately, secretly, and of its single choice disturb the peace of the world; or if it cannot be destroyed at present, at least its reduction to virtual impotency."

Because the Germans had held out so long before asking for peace and because of the vicious attack on the defenseless *Leinster*, Wilson insisted on harsher terms than before. He now called for the end of the German monarchy and a significant reduction in the power of the Junkers. Although Hindenburg had urged the chancellor to arrange for an armistice immediately, the threat to the throne seemed to him too great a price to pay. At Ludendorff's urging, Hindenburg suddenly declared the need to start another offensive.

The new chancellor, Prince Max of Baden, who had succeeded Count von Hertling on October 1, resisted the Supreme Command's arguments. He understood the strength of the Allies. He saw the weakening spirit of the German population in the cities. In Berlin an influenza epidemic was raging; on one day alone in October, more than 1,700 people died. Food was in short supply, and labor unrest was spreading. If the war did not soon end, an uprising would result.

Less than two years earlier, the military team of Hindenburg and Ludendorff had struggled with Chancellor Bethmann Hollweg over the question of submarine warfare. The generals had won, and Bethmann Hollweg was forced out of office. Once again, at the end of October 1918, Hindenburg opposed the position of a chancellor who was anxious to find a negotiated peace. On October 24 the military high command sent a telegram to all army units, ordering them to fight to the finish and denouncing the proposed conditions of the armistice as dishonorable. The idea of giving up territory in the east was more than Hindenburg could stand, and he blustered that Germany would fight to the last man. Although Hindenburg drafted the message, it was signed by Ludendorff. The telegram opposed the policy of the government and represented a direct challenge to the chancellor.

In the earlier conflict between military and civilian power, Hindenburg and Ludendorff had been able to overpower Chancellor Bethmann Hollweg. But in response to pressure from President Wilson, the kaiser had already committed Germany to a parliamentary government on September 29. At about the time of serious military setbacks for Germany in the Balkan Peninsula, the defensive Hindenburg (Siegfried) line on the western frontier was also broken. Now the chancellor had the upper hand. On October 26, two days after Hindenburg's telegram, the kaiser summoned the two generals. He rebuked Ludendorff for having sent orders to the army without first discussing the matter with the chancellor. The day before, Ludendorff had bellowed at the vice-chancellor that if the government did not do as he said, Germany would succumb to a communist revolution. Although Hindenburg, too, was responsible, he did not offer his resignation. Ludendorff resigned on the spot. Hindenburg did not attempt to stand in the way of Ludendorff's taking the blame. Their collaboration came to an abrupt conclusion. The stubborn and dictatorial Ludendorff was replaced by General Wilhelm Gröner.

On November 3, 1918, German sailors in the key

> *It must be a peace without victory. . . . Victory would mean peace forced upon the loser; a victor's terms upon the vanquished. It would be accepted in humiliation, under duress, at an intolerable sacrifice, and would leave a sting, a resentment, a bitter memory upon which terms of peace would rest not permanently, but only as upon quicksand.*
> —WOODROW WILSON
> U.S. president (1913–21), on January 22, 1917

British Prime Minister David Lloyd George, Italy's Baron Giorgio Sonnino, French Premier Georges Clemenceau, and U.S. President Wilson shaped the peace terms for World War I at the Versailles peace conference. After more U.S. citizens died as a result of Hindenburg's submarine campaign, Wilson toughened his stance, demanding the removal of the German monarchy.

port city of Kiel mutinied. Tired of the war and disappointed with the government's lack of progress in bringing about an armistice, they took matters into their own hands. They refused to continue serving in the imperial war machine. The constitutional monarchy had not come soon enough; military rule and a chancellor given power too late had only deepened Germany's difficulties. The uprising spread to other harbor cities, Hamburg, Dortmund, Bremen, and then to Mannheim, Munich, Nuremberg, Magdeburg. Revolutionary governments sprang up in Hanover, Brunswick, and Cologne. Power fell into the hands of *soviets*, or councils of radical workers and soldiers. In Munich, the capital of the kingdom of Bavaria, the royal dynasty was overthrown, and a soviet republic (modeled after the Russian Bolshevik system) was declared. Because the kaiser's government had not put an end to the war, the revolutionaries moved to put an end to the kaiser's government.

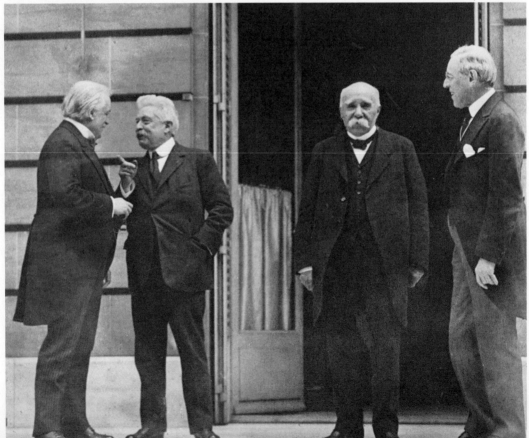

As the revolution spread, the leadership of the powerful Social Democratic party (the leading German socialist party) turned out to be a strong force opposed to revolution. It was loyal to the state and devoted to law and order. The Social Democratic leader, Friedrich Ebert, urged the kaiser to abdicate immediately in order to slow down the revolution. Prince Max of Baden, also hoping to stop radical forces from seizing control, called on the kaiser at least to promise abdication as soon as an armistice was reached. But the kaiser refused, hoping to lead his army against the revolution and to restore law and order in Germany. Hindenburg supported him. Once again, the military leader fostered an illusion, delaying urgently needed political action.

Germany must have her place in the sun.
—KAISER WILHELM II

On the morning of November 9 news reached Spa that a general strike had been called in Berlin, where mass demonstrations filled the streets. The Spartacist Karl Liebknecht, who wanted to overthrow "imperialist capitalists," was about to declare Berlin a revolutionary soviet. Mutiny was spreading through the military. At general headquarters, Hindenburg announced that he would ask the kaiser to abdicate. Yet the kaiser could not make a definite decision. He even agreed to give up his title as German emperor, while remaining king of Prussia. The state that had been founded at Versailles in 1871, in a ceremony witnessed by the young officer Hindenburg, was soon to be no more.

The compromise engineered by Prince Max and Hindenburg was too late. By the afternoon, messages arrived from Berlin describing the political confusion. Philipp Scheidemann, a Social Democrat and member of the chancellor's cabinet, had declared Germany a republic. That same day Ebert had been named chancellor by Prince Max. Ebert was shocked and angered to find he was the chancellor of a "republic." Scheidemann had consulted no one. The key issue in the capital was no longer the fate of the empire but whether Germany would be ruled by moderates or the revolutionaries. Previously the largest political force in the empire, the trade-union movement split in two. The middle-of-the-road Social Democrats and Majority Socialists (the founding German socialist party) were caught in a bitter struggle with the radicals, who wanted to imitate Lenin's Bolshevik revolution.

Fearing that the kaiser might be captured by the revolutionaries, Hindenburg and his officers decided that the emperor must flee to Holland. The army could not support him. After objecting to the suggestion, he finally gave in. When Hindenburg left him, late on November 9, it was the last time the field marshal and the emperor would meet. Early the next morning the imperial train sped toward the Dutch border.

Because of Hindenburg's inability to size up political situations accurately, Germany had continued to fight long after the war had been lost. Finally he recognized the need for an armistice. Similarly, his poor judgment had encouraged the kaiser to hold on to the throne until the revolution forced him out. In both cases, Hindenburg's change of heart had been too late. Subsequently, he would try to deny these belated insights and blame such blunders on those around him.

Nevertheless, the former emperor of the German Empire, exiled to the Castle of Doorn in Holland, accused Hindenburg of having forced his abdication. Hindenburg felt himself responsible for advising the kaiser to flee, and although he came to regret that advice, he was open to criticism from nationalist politicians.

After Prince Max declined Ebert's request that he stay on to help administer a new government, Ebert wondered what the army would do. The army remained Hindenburg's responsibility. Would it try to seize power in order to suppress the "Bolsheviks," or would it obey the new chancellor? General Gröner telephoned Ebert to inform him that Hindenburg had ordered the army to return to Germany. Hindenburg's only demands were that the chancellor support the army and military discipline. Gröner added that Hindenburg expected that the government would pledge to combat the anticapitalist revolutionaries.

On November 11, 1918, the armistice was signed and World War I at last came to a close. During the

> *The revolution of November 9th [1918] was chiefly a political revolution, whereas the real revolution must be chiefly an economic one.*
> —ROSA LUXEMBURG
> German socialist

ensuing months, the first German Republic, called the Weimar Republic after the city where a new National Assembly voted on the constitution in August 1919, fought for its survival against opponents on the right and on the left (conservatives who wanted to restore the old German Empire and those who wanted a revolutionary society). Ebert was elected by this assembly as the republic's first president.

The young republic, under the leadership of Ebert, the Social Democrat, depended heavily on the support of the army. Its constitution granted basic individual freedoms, universal suffrage, and most importantly, proportional representation in the assembly; thus the separation between the Prussian state and the rest of Germany was abolished. Meanwhile, the victors met in Paris and set forth harsh terms for the peace in the Treaty of Versailles. Hindenburg watched all these events, but he was no longer a central actor. He had commanded the German troops, lost the biggest war in human history, and failed his emperor. Hindenburg sent a letter of resignation to Ebert. Another was sent to the former kaiser in Holland, who had originally appointed him.

German peace delegates at Versailles, outside Paris, France, in 1919. It had been at Versailles that Hindenburg had witnessed the installation of Kaiser Wilhelm I as head of the unified German Empire in 1871. Always loyal to the emperor, Hindenburg was slow to recognize signs of Germany's defeat in 1918.

73

UPI/BETTMANN NEWSPHOTOS

In July 1919 Hindenburg retired to this house in Hanover, after sending letters of resignation to Wilhelm II, who blamed Hindenburg for his abdication, and to Ebert, who was elected president of the republic by the German National Assembly in the city of Weimar.

On July 4, 1919, Hindenburg returned to Hanover for the first time since that fateful morning in August 1914. He was greeted at the train station by the mayor and the city's dignitaries. A guard of honor stood at attention, and cheering crowds of citizens and soldiers lined the streets as the mayor accompanied him to a villa, a gift of the city to the returning hero.

Although the war had ended in defeat, the myth of Tannenberg flourished. Crowds regularly gathered in front of the Hindenburg residence and applauded whenever the field marshal came into view. He complained to his friends that he could never go shopping in the city because crowds of well-wishers would immediately gather around him.

Hindenburg returned to retirement and his favorite pastimes, hunting and collecting paintings. He had no political ambitions, and only rarely did he accept invitations to appear in public. He nevertheless made a major impact on German political life and severely weakened the stability of the new democracy. In November 1920 he visited Berlin to testify before a commission of inquiry investigating the history of imperial war policy. Accompanied by Ludendorff, Hindenburg claimed that the German army had not been defeated by foreign adversaries but by defeatist politicians and traitors at home.

This claim of treason came to be known as the *Dolchstoss,* or "stab in the back." The leaders of the republic came to be denounced as "November traitors." Because these leaders were socialists, they were lumped together with the revolutionaries in the minds of conservatives and nationalists. This feeling of betrayal grew worse when the terms imposed by the Allies created hardship. During the coming years, nationalist politicians would repeat the stab-in-the-back accusation in order to weaken public confidence in the republican government.

Hindenburg made this argument in his memoirs, which he finished in September 1919. In this book he attempted to defend himself against many of his critics, and he conspicuously avoided addressing many key allegations. It is the conclusion of the memoirs, however, that is most remarkable, for there the defeated hero of Tannenberg spelled out his political hopes, a return to the empire he had lost: ". . . from the tempestuous seas of our national life will once more emerge that rock — the German Imperial House — to which the hopes of our fathers clung in the days of yore." In 1919 no one yet knew how the eccentric political beliefs of this retired soldier, more than 70 years old, would soon shake the new republic.

> *The accusation that Germany was responsible for the greatest of all wars, we hereby repudiate. . . . With clean hearts we marched out to defend our Fatherland and with clean hands did we wield the sword.*
> —PAUL VON HINDENBURG
> at the Tannenberg
> memorial dedication

6

President von Hindenburg

When Hindenburg returned to Hanover in 1919 to begin his second retirement, he was 72 years old. His aversion to the new political arrangement grew even stronger. He was not friendly to the Weimar Republic. He rejected the very idea of democracy, and he opposed the new political leadership, full of the democratic radicals he had learned to fear long ago during his youth at Neudeck and in the Cadet Corps.

Though somewhat reclusive in his retirement, Hindenburg did occasionally appear in public. He attended, for example, the commemoration of the Battle of Tannenberg, and he had given testimony to the commission of inquiry in 1920. At these events, his hostility to the young democracy became evident. Soon the whole nation knew that the hero of Tannenberg would welcome a return to rule by the kaiser and the officer corps. Hindenburg no longer discussed the military developments that followed the Allied breakthrough at Amiens on August 8, 1918. Instead, he continued to maintain that the leadership of the new Weimar Republic was to blame for the shameful surrender.

Ebert saw from the beginning that the postwar chaos would breed riots, rebellions, and opportuni-

I have a great dislike for all this party politicking and parliamentary bickering. As a professional soldier I was accustomed always either to command or to obey.
—PAUL VON HINDENBURG

Still remembered as the hero of Tannenberg, Hindenburg is greeted by well-wishers in Schleswig-Holstein, Germany. In 1920 Hindenburg published his memoirs *Aus meinem Leben* (*Out of My Life*), in which he asserted that traitors had caused Germany's defeat in 1918.

Born to Jewish parents in Russian Poland, Rosa Luxemburg became a prominent German socialist who opposed all political support for the kaiser's war effort. She and the Spartacist leader, Karl Liebknecht, were murdered by government troops in January 1919.

ties for forces more radical than his own Social Democratic government. Volunteers from the army were recruited for an armed organization called the *Freikorps*. They were used to fight the Spartacists and to destroy the soviets in Munich and other cities. It was a group of these often cruel commandos who captured Rosa Luxemburg and Karl Liebknecht. The two socialists were beaten, then shot on January 15, 1919.

Nationalist extremists carried out a series of attacks on politicians involved with the republic. In August 1921 they assassinated Matthias Erzberger, a leader of the Center party (a moderate Catholic organization), because he had directed the German delegation that signed the armistice. From the nationalist perspective, that signature, which ended the bloodshed of World War I, amounted to an act of treason.

They also assassinated in 1922 the gifted foreign minister of the Weimar Republic, Walther Rathenau. Before November 1918 Rathenau had devoted himself to organizing the German supply systems during the war and had always vigorously supported the war effort. But as foreign minister of the Weimar Republic, Rathenau insisted on negotiating with Germany's former enemies, and the nationalists detested this policy. Moreover, Rathenau was Jewish, and the conservative opponents of the republic were viciously anti-Semitic. The extreme nationalists blamed the "treason" of November 1918 largely on the Catholics of the Center party, the radicals among the Social Democrats, and the members of the Communist party, founded by the Spartacists Luxemburg and Liebknecht in December 1918. But such accusations were especially focused on Jews.

Hindenburg himself did not actively agitate against the republic, but by publicly spreading the myth of a stab in the back, he undermined faith in the young state. More importantly, the nationalists claimed Hindenburg as one of their own and hoped to use him in order to overthrow the government. Hindenburg was a member of the *Stahlhelm* (Steel Helmet), an organization for German veterans. Unlike the Freikorps, the group did not engage in ter-

ror. However, it did consider the German republic to be the result of a "swinish revolution," and it was even outlawed in parts of Germany. In December 1919 a right-wing officer, Colonel Max Bauer, Ludendorff's former aide, told an American journalist that "we intend to restore the monarchy on the English model, and the election of Hindenburg would help us to that end." A month later, Pastor Traub, another opponent of the republic, said that Hindenburg "is not a man who would bar the way to a future kaiser; on the contrary, he would prepare it."

The opportunity seemed to present itself to abolish the first German democracy. The Versailles Treaty strictly limited the size of the German army. The German government therefore ordered the abolition of certain military units. The commanders of these units refused to obey their orders and began to march on Berlin in order to overthrow the government. When the president, Ebert, called upon the head of the army, General Hans von Seeckt, to put down the mutiny, the general turned down the order. The general said that German soldiers would not fire on members of their own army even if they were attacking the government.

The army was still commanded by officers who had sworn their loyalty to the kaiser. They would

Outraged citizens of the Weimar Republic rally in Berlin to protest the assassination by German nationalist extremists of Foreign Minister Walther Rathenau in 1922. Rathenau, who was Jewish, had overseen the supplying of the German army during World War I, but was later targeted by nationalists as a "traitor."

79

not come to the defense of the republic. The government fled Berlin, while the mutinous troops, which included Colonel Max Bauer, occupied the capital on March 13. The incident has come to be known as the Kapp *Putsch* (revolt), after one of its leaders, Wolfgang Kapp.

From its temporary headquarters in Stuttgart, the republic called on the workers of Berlin to resist the sudden military rebellion by stopping all work. Within four days, the Kapp putsch was defeated, thanks to the loyalty of the Berlin population to the Weimar Republic. Nevertheless, the putsch showed that there were many government officials who were in league with individuals hostile to democracy. They wanted the kaiser to return to Germany. They did not regard the republic as a truly German form of government but only as a model imposed on Germany by Great Britain, France, Italy, and the United

German sentries stand guard on the Rhine River. Immediately after the war, the democratic government in Germany was threatened by revolutionaries influenced by Lenin, the Russian Bolshevik leader. Extreme right-wing nationalists also posed a danger to the republic.

States. Other members of the old aristocracy favored a renewed monarchy headed by Crown Prince Rupprecht of Bavaria. The republic was a sign of the defeat in the war.

Meanwhile, the Communist party, which took the place of the Spartacists, denounced the Social Democrats. German communists looked forward to a Soviet-style revolution. In 1923 French troops occupied the Ruhr Valley, Germany's industrial center. Clashes between these forces and the Germans caused many to think another war would erupt. The French blockaded the area known as the Rhineland, increasing unrest in Germany.

To make matters still worse, inflation was destroying the value of German money. In 1923 the pressure on the German economy to pay the Allied nations for damages caused by the war had helped create a terrifying economic crisis. In the summer of 1914 an American dollar had been worth about 4 German marks; by the end of 1923 it was worth billions. Inflation increased so rapidly that workers were paid several times a day, since prices would be higher in the evening than they had been that morning. The savings of the middle class were depleted. Literally billions of dollars in German currency were needed simply to buy a newspaper. To the communists, it seemed the moment was right to rebel and form revolutionary governments in Hamburg and the states of Saxony and Thuringia.

In November a pistol-waving Adolf Hitler led his militant nationalist organization in the "beer hall putsch" in the Bavarian city of Munich. Hitler's party was called the National Socialist German Workers' party, or the *Nazis*. Though the word "socialist" was in their name, the Nazis did not believe in socialism. The Social Democrats, in fact, were their enemies. They favored a dictatorship that would lead to a rearmed, powerful German state. Resorting to street violence to get their way, Hitler's followers blamed Jews, communists, and non-Germans for Germany's defeat and subsequent economic suffering.

Fearing the spread of political radicalism in central Europe, the U. S. government decided to aid the German economy in 1924. A program was intro-

Adolf Hitler's extremist National Socialist German Workers' party, or Nazis, on parade in Munich, Germany, in 1923. A decade later, Hitler became Nazi dictator of Germany. In 1925 Hindenburg reluctantly became a candidate for the presidency of the Weimar Republic, and won, with the support of the German National People's party.

> I have always pledged unbounded loyalty to my Kaiser, King and Lord, and will always do so.
>
> —PAUL VON HINDENBURG

duced to ease the repayment of the war debt — the so-called Dawes Plan, named after the U.S. financier Charles G. Dawes. Large loans helped the German economy to get back on its feet. Major construction projects were undertaken, producing jobs and alleviating the housing shortage. In addition, through the leadership of skillful German statesman Gustav Stresemann, Germany's diplomatic relations with its European neighbors improved. Finally the Weimar Republic became more stable, and the nationalist threat to democracy began to subside.

This recovery was due in part to the influence of Friedrich Ebert. A leader of the moderate wing of the Social Democratic party, Ebert was technically considered the last chancellor of the German Empire but was the first *Reichspräsident* of the republic. He had defended the government against its opponents. He oversaw Germany's return to normal diplomatic relations, and he helped overcome the economic turmoil. Ebert devoted himself to the new democracy and became the symbol of the Weimar Republic.

On February 28, 1925, Ebert died. According to the Weimar constitution, a new election had to be held within a month. The election was based on a "common, equal, direct, and secret vote" in which all citizens, male and female, above the age of 20 could participate. If no candidate received an absolute majority of the votes cast, a second ballot would be necessary.

The controversy and dissension that promised to accompany the election threatened to disrupt political life. The defenders of the republic understood that their opponents were eager to elect a president who would dismantle the democracy and return Germany to the kaiser. Yet neither the supporters of the democrats nor the nationalists were able to unite around single candidates. Consequently, seven different candidates ran in the election.

The election took place on March 29, 1925. Some (but not all) conservative groups had agreed to support the mayor of Duisburg, Dr. Karl Jarres, who received the most votes. However, he received no majority. Together, the moderate Otto Braun of the Social Democrats and Wilhelm Marx of the Center party had nearly 2 million more votes than the conservative Jarres. The Communist party's candidate, Ernst Thälmann, received 1.9 million, and Ludendorff, representing Hitler's Nazi party, had the least, with 280,000. A new election was necessary.

Three parties on the left grouped together in defense of the new state. This "Weimar Block," composed of Social Democrats, the Center, and the Democratic parties, supported Marx. The Communist party did not cooperate, however, and insisted again on running its own candidate. Who would be the candidate of the right-wing nationalists?

There was no obvious choice. Some, eager for a return to monarchy, proposed a member of the kaiser's family as candidate. Others preferred a representative of heavy industry. Still others wanted an important military figure in the public eye, such as General von Seeckt. A week passed with no decision, until the leader of the nationalist delegation from Hanover hit on an exciting idea—Hindenburg.

As early as 1920, after having settled into his second retirement, Hindenburg had been asked not to rule out becoming a candidate. He had issued a statement saying he would "accept an eventual presidential election, in case this should be the wish of the people in the Fatherland." The fabled hero of Tannenberg was still immensely popular. His belief in the stab-in-the-back myth and his open loyalty to the kaiser appealed to the nationalists. They counted on Hindenburg to bring down the democratic regime. They also knew of Hindenburg's sense of personal guilt for the flight of the kaiser and hoped to exploit this.

When Hindenburg was first approached, he resisted the idea. He was an old man spending his days in a well-deserved retirement. Moreover, he was a soldier who had always disliked politics, especially the complex political rules of a democracy. The suggestion that Hindenburg run for the presidency of the republic was a strange one.

On April 6 Admiral Alfred von Tirpitz, a former secretary of the navy, now a representative to the

Worthless German currency is packed and baled in a junk shop. By 1923, payments demanded from Germany by the Allied nations placed great pressure on the unstable German economy. Severe inflation rapidly destroyed the buying power of German money.

A procession representing the campaign to elect Hindenburg president of the Weimar Republic passes the presidential palace. When no clear winner emerged from the March 1925 election, the still popular Hindenburg was persuaded to run. In April he defeated the candidates of the Catholic Center and Communist parties.

Reichstag for the German National People's party, or German Nationalists, visited Hindenburg in Hanover. He knew exactly how to appeal to the general. Hindenburg should run for the presidency, he argued, but he should not represent any special interest or political party. Hindenburg should stand above politics. He must serve Germany. His nation was calling on him once again in an hour of crisis, and Hindenburg, with his soldierly sense of duty, was persuaded.

Throughout the campaign, Hindenburg faced a deep conflict. He had sworn his loyalty to the kaiser and the German Empire; now he was agreeing to serve the democratic state. Of course, the nationalists hoped he would help dismantle the democracy. But he had to convince himself as well as the electorate that he was a genuine candidate.

Hindenburg explained this difficult position in an Easter message at the height of the campaign: "My life lies open to all the world. I believe that in time of need I have done my duty. If this duty were to bid me now as president of the Reich to work within the articles of the Constitution, without respect for party, persons, origin, or profession, I shall not be found wanting. As a soldier, I have always had the whole nation before my eyes, and not its parties."

Hindenburg suggested that even though he personally found the democratic constitution not to his liking, he could honorably promise to defend it, since the president, he maintained, should stand above politics. In the election of 1925, Hindenburg decided faithfully to perform his external duties to the republic, while promising to keep his personal, antidemocratic beliefs to himself.

The second vote took place on Sunday, April 26, 1925. By Monday the results were in. Hindenburg was victorious with 14,655,766 votes. Wilhelm Marx, who had been chancellor from 1923 to 1924, received 13,751,615, and Ernst Thälmann received 1,931,151. If the Communist party had voted with the other leftist parties, Marx would have won; the split between the Social Democrats and the communists helped the right-wing German Nationalists win the election. Most of Marx's support was in the cities, whereas in the agricultural regions where the Junkers still influenced the electorate, Hindenburg was the winner. Hindenburg had also benefited from prejudices against Marx, the Catholic candidate, in parts of Prussia, Thuringia, and Saxony, where Protestants were in the majority.

On May 11 the president-elect left Hanover and traveled to Berlin, where he was greeted by jubilant crowds. The thunderous applause reminded him of the crowds that had applauded the victorious soldiers in 1866 and 1871. Although some of his nationalist supporters had hoped that the monarchist Hindenburg would refuse to take an oath to defend the democratic constitution, he had agreed to participate in the ceremony. On May 12 he stood before the legislature, raised his hand, and spoke clearly: "I swear by God, the Almighty and the All-knowing, that I will devote my powers to the welfare of the German people, increase its benefits, turn danger from it, guard the Constitution and the Laws of the Reich, conscientiously fulfill my duties, and do justice towards everyone, so help me God."

7

The President and the Republic

Less than a week after his inauguration, President von Hindenburg met the foreign minister, Gustav Stresemann, who had also served as chancellor in 1923. Stresemann was a strong advocate of the "Policy of Fulfillment." Fulfillment meant recognizing Germany's defeat in the world war and the necessity of complying with the demands of the victors. He, too, wanted to see foreign troops leave Germany. Stresemann understood that only this policy could establish greater stability among nations, reduce Germany's war debts, and solve the nation's serious economic problems. There were fears outside of Germany that Hindenburg's presidency would clear the way for a renewed monarchy and that in the meantime the former kaiser would simply dictate policy from nearby Holland.

Because Stresemann argued for the importance of friendly ties with France, Great Britain, and the United States, he was bitterly attacked by conservative and nationalist politicians. The basic assumptions of his Policy of Fulfillment directly opposed the nationalist doctrine of the stab in the back. Foreign Minister Stresemann feared that the new president would swiftly demolish all his delicate diplomatic work with the Allies.

Stresemann was surprised by his first meeting with the president. Hindenburg listened attentively

In this festive first hour I summon the whole population to work with me. My office and my aim do not belong to a single class, not to one race or to one religion, but rather to the whole German nation and all its members, bound together by its harsh fate.
—PAUL VON HINDENBURG
after his election as
president, in 1925

Paul von Hindenburg as president of the German Weimar Republic. Shortly after World War I, Hindenburg had written that "from the seas of our national life will . . . emerge that rock — the German Imperial House." But in 1925 he pledged to defend the republic's constitution.

as the diplomat explained his plans and described the need for friendly relations with the Allied powers. The president was soon persuaded that reconciliation and the Policy of Fulfillment were in the German national interest. He had refrained from putting forward the aggressive views of his nationalist supporters.

In fact, Hindenburg could not understand why this devoted public servant, who could argue so well for his policies, designed to benefit Germany, could provoke such anger among the conservatives. So at the close of the interview, Hindenburg turned to the foreign minister and asked, "If things are as you say, why are you always so furiously attacked?" Stresemann replied, "I have frequently asked myself that same question."

In order to strengthen Germany's international position, Stresemann proceeded with reconciliation. Conservative forces were hostile both to the United States and the European democracies. They resented the attempt to make Germany more democratic and considered Stresemann their enemy. De-

The brilliant Foreign Minister Gustav Stresemann, who served as chancellor in 1923, addresses the League of Nations, the international organization formed after World War I. Stresemann advocated a "Policy of Fulfillment" regarding Germany's treaty obligations after the world war, a position Hindenburg came to support.

spite their hopes that the hero of Tannenberg would end the Policy of Fulfillment and the Weimar Republic, Hindenburg had taken an oath to defend the republic, and he allowed Stresemann to continue his negotiations.

These negotiations led to Stresemann's greatest achievement, the Treaty of Locarno, which was signed in October 1925. The basic principle of the treaty involved an agreement between Germany, France, and Belgium to recognize their mutual borders. This recognition included a final renunciation of German claims to certain Belgian territories and especially the French provinces of Alsace and Lorraine. Germany had conquered these territories in the Franco-Prussian War, and they had been returned to France after the signing of the Versailles Treaty in June 1919.

German nationalists voiced outrage over this surrender of Alsace and Lorraine, but in exchange, Stresemann won the withdrawal of British troops from German territory, the Rhineland. In March 1926 Hindenburg was able to travel to Cologne, now free of foreign troops. There he was greeted by enthusiastic crowds.

Because of the Treaty of Locarno and Stresemann's efforts, a new era of peace seemed to be guaranteed for Europe. In the fall of 1926 Germany entered the League of Nations. As a permanent

Members of the German Nationalists, with their leader, the bespectacled Alfred Hugenberg (far right). Although the German Nationalists convinced Hindenburg to run for president of the Weimar Republic, they later denounced him for paying reparations to the nations that had defeated Germany.

member of the league's council, Germany was accorded the rank of a great power. Another triumph was a treaty with the Soviet Union, signed in Berlin in April 1926 and approved by all German parties, even on the right. This treaty built upon an earlier agreement reached at Rapallo, Italy, by the Weimar government and Soviet Ambassador Georgi Chicherin. Thanks to Stresemann, the Weimar Republic was able to restore to Germany much of the international respect that the German Empire had lost during World War I. As foreign minister, Stresemann was the architect of this transformation. Yet his success was due in large part to Hindenburg's support.

While the Treaty of Locarno had eased much of the bitterness lingering after the war, there were still cries for justice. The Hohenzollerns, the family of the deposed kaiser, and other aristocrats who had fallen from power continued to demand financial support from the republic. In response, the left-wing

Unemployed workers in Austria during the Great Depression of the 1930s. Stresemann's negotiations, approved by President Hindenburg, won needed foreign investment through the U.S.-sponsored Dawes Plan. When the New York Stock Exchange plummeted, so did Germany's economy, resulting in widespread unemployment.

parties introduced a bill to seize the property of the nobility.

The socialists argued that the aristocrats had profited long enough from the German people. Did not the nation have a right to reclaim its wealth from the kaiser? On the other hand, moderates and conservatives insisted on the need to respect the private property of everyone, including Wilhelm II. A national vote on the issue was held in June 1926, and the proposed expropriation received massive support.

Since Hindenburg considered it his duty as president to stand above political debate, he refused to take a public position on this proposal. However, after the vote he wrote a letter to the chairman of his election committee in which he expressed his displeasure with the outcome: "That I, who have spent my life in the service of the Prussian kings and the German emperors, feel this referendum primarily as a great injustice, and also as an exhibition of a regrettable lack of traditional sentiment and of great ingratitude, I do not need to explain to you. The very foundation of a constitutional state is the legal recognition of property, and the proposal of expropriation offends against the principles of morality and justice. . . . I trust therefore that our fellow citizens will reconsider their decision on this matter, and will undo the mischief they have done."

Hindenburg had expressed this opinion, defending the rights of the imperial family, in a private letter. But conservative allies of the former kaiser made quick use of the letter. They reprinted it as a poster that was hung on kiosks throughout the country. Another vote was taken, and this time the proposed expropriation was defeated. In addition, the Hohenzollerns were granted extensive landholdings, many castles, and 15 million gold marks.

Hindenburg disappointed his conservative supporters by giving his approval to Stresemann's Policy of Fulfillment. He pleased these same conservatives by not taking away the imperial family's property. He also pleased the conservatives by ordering that German embassies abroad should fly

UPI/BETTMANN NEWSPHOTOS

Adolf Hitler in Tyrolian mountain dress. Hitler's Nazis challenged six other parties in March 1925 for the presidency of the Weimar Republic but fared poorly. Two years earlier, Hitler, whose party stood for violent nationalism and racism, staged the Beer Hall putsch in Munich, Germany.

both the new flag of the republic and the old flag of the German Empire. These symbols indicate how Hindenburg, even as president of the republic, remained loyal to the imperial past.

Yet Hindenburg's symbolic gestures had little influence on Weimar politics. After the republic's turbulent first four years, the Dawes Plan and the Treaty of Locarno in 1925 allowed the German economy to thrive, especially when U.S. investments began pouring into Germany. For a time, inflation seemed under control, and unemployment figures fell.

Much of the population came to appreciate the achievements of the republic and withdrew their

Flanked by government officials, Hindenburg attends the funeral in 1929 of Gustav Stresemann. The foreign minister had worked tirelessly to revitalize Germany's economy and normalize its diplomatic relations during the 1920s.

support from the right-wing nationalists. In May 1928 elections for the Reichstag were held. The conservative parties were soundly defeated. A government was formed under the leadership of the Social Democratic Chancellor Hermann Müller. His cabinet included members of the People's party, the Center party, and another party, called the Democrats.

The first German democracy, the Weimar Republic, appeared to be standing on solid ground. But this stability was merely an illusion. Soon after the 1928 elections, three factors began to undermine the republic: political intrigue, a foreign policy debate, and a world economic crisis. Because of his reluctance to engage in politics, Hindenburg failed to provide effective aid to the state he had sworn to defend. He delayed too long in taking active measures on the republic's behalf; the repercussions contributed to the rapid decline of the democratic system.

The German Nationalists, led by the publisher Alfred Hugenberg, drew up a resolution in September 1928. Its words were violent: "We hate the present form of the German state with all our hearts because it denies us the hope of freeing our enslaved Fatherland, of cleansing the German people of the war-guilt lie." The term "war guilt" referred to a clause in the Treaty of Versailles concerning German reparations demanded by the Allies. It stated that Germany accepted "responsibility . . . for causing all the loss and damage" the Allied governments had experienced during World War I.

Nevertheless, the Social Democrats remained the big winners in 1928. They were not radicals. On the contrary, since 1919 Social Democratic policy had strived to establish a stable democracy with a healthy economy. Nevertheless, they were deeply distrusted by conservatives in the German army, where the traditions of imperial officers still flourished. Because of his background, Hindenburg was particularly susceptible to the influence of the army. One of the officers who influenced Hindenburg, General Kurt von Schleicher, later plotted against General Gröner and a future chancellor. He looked forward to an opportunity to put an end to the Social

In a radio broadcast to the world in 1932, Hindenburg explains Germany's plight during the Great Depression. Nationalists, who had supported Hindenburg hoping that he would dismantle democracy and oppose cooperation with Great Britain, France, and the United States, attacked the president for tying the German economy to U.S. investments.

UPI/BETTMANN NEWSPHOTOS

A street sweeper in Prussia cleans up campaign leaflets after general elections in 1930, in which the Nazi party made huge gains. The Nazis, whose views were similar to those of Italian fascist dictator Benito Mussolini, advocated a one-party government ruled by a single leader.

Democratic government and to replace the parliamentary system with his own authority. Eventually, Schleicher, too, became chancellor.

As Hindenburg fell increasingly under such influences, foreign policy once again was being hotly debated. The Dawes Plan had provided only a temporary arrangement for payment of the German war debt. In 1929 Foreign Minister Stresemann was busy negotiating a final agreement that came to be known as the Young Plan. The Young Plan promised a full evacuation of the Rhineland by June 1930. With no more foreign troops stationed on German soil, the nation had regained its independence. The Young Plan, just as importantly, made the schedule for reparations payments more lenient, with annual payments lasting until 1988.

Again the Policy of Fulfillment was the topic of debate, and the conservative nationalists again opposed any concession. Hugenberg, who owned many newspapers, used his extensive control of the press to carry on a campaign against the Young Plan and, ultimately, against the republic itself.

Hugenberg supported a referendum, or popular vote, to introduce a "Bill against the Enslavement of the German People" in the Reichstag. With Hitler's Nazis, the German Nationalists wanted to put a stop to all payments to the Allies and consider any German chancellor guilty of treason for continuing such payments. To succeed, the referendum needed support of 10 percent of the electorate. A vote was held on November 3, 1929, and Hugenberg's initiative was approved by 10.2 percent, but it was thoroughly defeated in the legislature.

Hindenburg was pleased to see that his country was gradually becoming stronger and that foreign powers were finally departing. Theodor Heuss, the future German president, praised Hindenburg that year for his "well-disposed objectivity."

In January 1930 Chancellor Hermann Müller accepted the Young Plan. It still had to be ratified by President Hindenburg. Because Hindenburg made it known that he would sign the bill, as he was required by the constitution to do, he was denounced in the right-wing press. One nationalist newspaper wrote that Hindenburg "has today forfeited the unlimited confidence originally reposed in him by every genuinely patriotic German." Elsewhere he was threatened with assassination, the fate that Erzberger and Rathenau had met earlier in the decade.

When Hindenburg finally gave his official approval to the Young Plan, his former comrade Ludendorff, now a nationalist agitator, remarked: "Field Marshal von Hindenburg has forfeited the right to wear the field-gray uniform of the army and to be buried in it. Herr Paul von Hindenburg has destroyed the very thing he fought for as Field-Marshal."

The debate over the Young Plan marked a turning point in Hindenburg's career. In 1925 he had been elected with the support of the conservative German National People's party and the People's party against the candidate of the moderates and the left. When he approved the Young Plan, he was opposed by the German nationalists and supported by their opponents. His former supporters were now his enemies, and his former enemies were now his defenders.

Yet while the foreign policy debate continued to rage, a new crisis shook the very foundations of the Weimar Republic. Since the Dawes Plan of 1925, the German economy had come to rely on U.S. investments. In October 1929 the New York stock market fell into the greatest decline in its history. The crash led to the Great Depression in the United States, which set off a chain reaction of economic disaster worldwide. Germany's economic boom was short-lived. Disaster had struck. Unemployment increased drastically. By December 1931 there were 5,615,000 unemployed.

This unemployment disaster meant the spread of poverty. It also threw the German government into a financial crisis. Political extremists saw their chance to increase their power. Müller's government was now virtually helpless because the Social Democrats refused to accept the proposal of the other coalition parties to refuse unemployment insurance payments. On March 27, 1930, Müller resigned as

"Decide the future of your children. Vote for Hindenburg," a poster proclaims during the second vote in 1932, in which Hindenburg received a majority over Hitler. Combining electoral politics with street violence, the Nazis continued to gain strength in the Reichstag.

chancellor. Hindenburg promptly appointed a politician who had the strong support of the military: Heinrich Brüning of the Center party. Brüning, who had been in the army during World War I, said of becoming chancellor that he could not resist "the President's appeal to my soldier's sense of duty."

Brüning proposed to solve the financial crisis with a severe program that combined tax increases and sharp cutbacks in government spending. His plan was defeated in the Reichstag on July 16.

Brüning's policies marked the beginning of the end for the Weimar Republic. When Communists, Nazis, the German Nationalists, and even Social Democrats in the Reichstag refused to overcome their disagreements and turned down his economic proposals, Brüning instituted his own economic program by decree. Hindenburg, who believed the national interest was above parliamentary "bickering," approved using Article 48 of the Weimar Constitution. The article granted the president extraordinary emergency powers. While these powers were originally meant to apply only to military emergencies, Brüning, supported by Hindenburg, used the article to rule without a parliamentary majority. This arrangement was referred to as a "parliamentary presidential government." He later dissolved the Reichstag and set elections for September.

Though Brüning worked hard to save the republic, Hitler's Nazi toughs were now beating on the gates of power. The end of the republic came even closer when the results of the elections of September 14, 1930, became known. In 1928 Adolf Hitler's Nazi party had received 809,800 votes and 12 seats in the Reichstag; in 1930 the Nazis collected 6,406,379 votes and 107 seats. The economic crisis had produced widespread dissatisfaction with the Weimar system, and the Nazis, extreme right-wing opponents of democracy, were the winners.

During the following year, the situation became even worse. Unemployment continued to rise, and Brüning's strict policies earned him the nickname of the "Hunger Chancellor." His use of Article 48 contributed to a growing loss of faith in parliamentary rule. Strikes and terrorism became frequent, and street fighting repeatedly broke out between Nazi storm troopers, as they were known, and communists. Hitler replaced Hugenberg as the leader of the right-wing opposition to the Weimar system.

In 1932 Hindenburg's seven-year term as president was due to expire, but he again was convinced to run by an appeal to his sense of duty. He would have preferred a Reichstag vote to extend his term of office, but Brüning could not organize enough support. A bitter campaign ensued. Hindenburg, the Protestant Prussian, sympathetic to the past, was supported by the Catholic Center party, the Social Democratic workers, the unions, and Jewish citizens. His opponent, Hitler, originally a Catholic from Austria, was backed by industrialists, Protestant conservatives, and the rural population. The princes, members of the old aristocratic order, regarded Hindenburg as a traitor. A newspaper that had supported Hindenburg in 1925 now wrote: "The present issue at the polls is whether internationalist traitors and pacifist swine, with the approval of Hindenburg, are to bring about the final ruin of Germany."

Hindenburg won the election on March 13, 1932, but without an absolute majority. A second vote took place on April 10. Hindenburg received 53 percent, with 19,359,642 votes, against 13,417,460 for Hitler and 3,706,388 for the Communist party candidate, Thälmann. Hindenburg remained the president. In 1925 he had been elected by conservatives to destroy the republic and undermine its constitution. In 1932 he was elected by the moderates and socialists to defend the republic against the growing Nazi threat. The Weimar Republic had received one last chance, with Hindenburg at the helm.

UPI/BETTMANN NEWSPHOTOS

"With him," a poster proclaims, during the 1932 campaign. This was to be the last presidential election for the 84-year-old Hindenburg.

8

From Democracy to Dictatorship

The results of the election of April 10, 1932, were absolutely clear. Again, a majority of the voters had chosen Hindenburg for a second term as president of the Weimar Republic. Hitler had not yet won his bid for power.

The campaign had been very bitter, and nearly half the electorate had voted against him. This hurt Hindenburg, who thought of himself as a representative of the entire nation, standing above the quarreling parties. He was disturbed by the fact that the conservatives and nationalists had opposed him. He was uncomfortable with the support he received from socialists, democrats, and liberals, the groups he had disliked since his youth.

Hindenburg directed his displeasure toward Chancellor Brüning. Brüning had not convinced the Reichstag to extend Hindenburg's term of office, and this embarrassed the president. Brüning also assumed he could rely on the Social Democrats for support in the Reichstag. Hindenburg distrusted the Social Democrats, however.

In April Brüning banned the Nazi storm troopers, or Brown Shirts, because they used violence against Hitler's opponents. The nationalists protested Brü-

We are the result of the distress for which the others are responsible.
—ADOLF HITLER
German chancellor,
in 1933

With Chancellor Hitler and Hermann Göring nearby, Hindenburg visits the Tannenberg monument in 1934, commemorating the German victory there during World War I. As president of the German Republic, Hindenburg was convinced that he could rise above disputes between political parties.

UPI/BETTMANN NEWSPHOTOS

A young schoolboy wears the uniform of the Nazi storm troopers. This organization, which was composed of disaffected World War I veterans, hoodlums, and nationalists, attacked the Nazis' opponents in the streets. The Nazis' disruptive tactics worked: Hindenburg appointed Hitler chancellor in January 1933.

That man [Hitler] for chancellor? I'll make him postmaster, and he can lick the stamps with my head on them.
—PAUL VON HINDENBURG
in 1932

ning's decision, and Hindenburg was blamed for the chancellor's policy. The relationship of the president and his chancellor worsened.

Rule by presidential decree had undermined the principle of the democratic system. On May 29 Hindenburg told Brüning that he could no longer count on these powers. Brüning resigned the next day. Following General Schleicher's advice, Hindenburg appointed Franz von Papen as chancellor on June 1, 1932.

Papen was a right-wing politician of the Center party. He had the support of Schleicher, and he was an influential member of a conservative group of wealthy industrialists and the aristocracy. In 1916 he had worked in the German embassy in Washington, but he was expelled from the United States because he was involved in spying. Although Hindenburg had been elected by the left in April, he decided to appoint a right-wing government in June.

Like Brüning, Papen had no majority in the Reichstag. He had to rely on Article 48 and on the temporary support of the Nazis. His cabinet included many ministers from the old nobility, and it was promptly labeled the "Cabinet of Barons." Hindenburg was delighted. The government was now in the hands of the same elite groups that had prevailed before 1918. The democratic groups that had come to power during the revolution were ousted.

Papen's government faced two problems. First, Papen had excluded the Social Democrats from the national government, but the Social Democrats were still active in regional governments of the states (or *Länder*) — especially in the largest state, Prussia, whose government had been in the hands of Premier Otto Braun, a socialist, since 1919. Berlin, the capital of Germany, was also the capital of Prussia. The Prussian police force was very strong, and it was known to sympathize with the Social Democrats. Papen would not be able to carry out his plans unless he first controlled Prussia.

Despite their political differences, Braun thought that Hindenburg would save Germany from Hitler.

Hindenburg also knew the chief of police in Berlin, Albert Grzesinski. Long ago, in November 1918, Grzesinski, another socialist, who also served as Prussian minister of the interior, had publicly praised Hindenburg for helping to end World War I.

But the conservatives around Papen convinced Hindenburg that Braun's government was a threat to national security. Hindenburg approved the conservative plan: on July 20, 1932, the national government took over the Prussian state and ousted the socialists.

In the Kapp putsch of 1920, soldiers had marched into Berlin and tried to topple the democratic government. The Social Democrats had then called for a general strike, and the rebels had been quickly defeated. In 1932 the socialists of Prussia bowed to the authority of Hindenburg and the abolition of their government. In the coming months, Hitler and his Nazis would gain power and carry out their terrible plans.

Having abolished the left-wing government of Prussia, the Papen government faced the growing strength of the brutal Nazi movement. Hindenburg and Papen hoped to establish a stable, authoritarian regime, limit democracy, and perhaps have an emperor once more.

The Nazis were an even greater threat to democracy. Hitler's followers pinned all blame for Germany's difficulties on the communists, on other political opponents, and especially the Jews. Even many conservatives were frightened by the Nazis, since they also hated the princely landowning classes. Their program would put the government almost completely in charge of the economy. The Nazis were a fascist political organization. Benito Mussolini had established the first fascist state in Italy in 1925–26. Fascism is a political system that opposes individual freedoms. A fascist government is led by a single absolute dictator who permits only his own political party to exist. Both Italian and German fascists advocated military aggression and conquest. Hitler's Nazis were violently nationalistic. They believed in the myth of a pure Germanic race.

The day when [the Nazis] were a vital threat is gone. . . . It is not unlikely that Hitler will end his career as an old man in some Bavarian village who, in the Tiergarten in the evening, tells his intimates how he nearly overturned the German Reich.
—HAROLD LASKI
British socialist, in 1932

Members of Hitler's cabinet. Top row, left to right: Vice-Chancellor Franz von Papen, Wilhelm Frick, Baron Konstantin von Neurath. Second row: Alfred Hugenberg, Count Lutz Schwerin-Krosigk, Franz Seldte, General Werner von Blomberg. Third row: Baron Paul Eltz von Rubenach, Hermann Göring, Günther Gerecke, and Dr. Funk.

After weakening the Social Democrats, Papen planned to undermine the Nazis by offering them power. By making concessions to Hitler and inviting him into the government, Papen thought he could put the Nazis under his control. The plan backfired.

Soon after his appointment as chancellor, Papen revoked Brüning's ban on the Nazi storm troopers, who terrorized those considered to be the enemies of the Nazi movement. The decision was an open invitation to political murder. In June and July the Nazi Brown Shirts provoked hundreds of street battles. In Prussia alone, 99 people were killed and more than 1,000 wounded.

Hitler won a big victory in the Reichstag election of July 31. The Nazis' representation increased from 107 seats to 230. As the leader of the largest party, Hitler felt he deserved to be appointed chancellor.

But Hindenburg offered him only the vice-chancellorship. If Hitler accepted, he would have been under Papen's conservative control. Hitler refused.

New elections were held in November. Hitler's popularity was beginning to decline. Again Hindenburg offered to appoint him vice-chancellor. Again Hitler refused. The crisis in the Reichstag continued. Papen's conservative government needed to have majority support in the Reichstag. This was not possible without the Nazis' participation, and the Nazis refused to participate unless Hitler was named chancellor. Yet Hindenburg and the conservatives did not want to turn over full power to him; they wanted to find a way to control him. Hindenburg told Hitler in a letter why he could not appoint him: "A party led by you would force its way to a party dictatorship." Hindenburg said that he could not make such an appointment because it would violate his oath of loyalty and his conscience.

In December Papen was replaced by General Schleicher. Yet Schleicher, too, failed to find a solution. On January 30, 1933, Hindenburg took the fateful step. He appointed Adolf Hitler as chancellor of Germany. Papen became vice-chancellor. New elections were planned for March.

Hindenburg thought that Papen would still be able to block Hitler's plans. But on February 4 Hindenburg signed a presidential decree allowing the prohibition of meetings and newspapers that "abused, or treated with contempt, organs, institutions, bureaus or leading officials of this state." The decree allowed the new Nazi minister of the interior, Hermann Göring, to suppress anti-Nazi newspapers. The Nazis' political opponents now did not have a fair chance in the parliamentary election. Meanwhile, the chief Nazi propagandist, Josef Goebbels, made use of the state-controlled radio by broadcasting Hitler's speeches.

On February 17 Göring ordered the police, who were now under his command, to cooperate with the storm troopers. Socialists, communists, Jews, and others were arrested without hearings. On February 27 the Reichstag building was destroyed by a fire. Although the fire was probably set by a Nazi group, the Nazis blamed it on the communists.

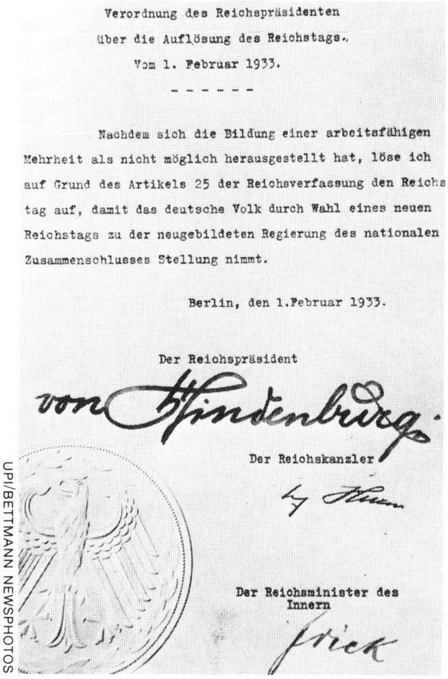
Verordnung des Reichspräsidenten
über die Auflösung des Reichstags.
Vom 1. Februar 1933.

Nachdem sich die Bildung einer arbeitsfähigen Mehrheit als nicht möglich herausgestellt hat, löse ich auf Grund des Artikels 25 der Reichsverfassung den Reichstag auf, damit das deutsche Volk durch Wahl eines neuen Reichstags zu der neugebildeten Regierung des nationalen Zusammenschlusses Stellung nimmt.

Berlin, den 1.Februar 1933.

Der Reichspräsident
von Hindenburg

Der Reichskanzler

Der Reichsminister des Innern
Frick

UPI/BETTMANN NEWSPHOTOS

President Hindenburg and Chancellor Hitler signed this order dissolving the Reichstag in February 1933. Hitler had won his position as chancellor as the price for Nazi cooperation with the republic. Hitler's predecessors Papen and Schleicher had failed to control the Nazis.

THE NEW YORK PUBLIC LIBRARY

Hitler and Papen on their way to the Reichstag, then under Nazi control, on March 21, 1933, following the fire there for which the Nazis were probably responsible. In February Hindenburg had helped the Nazis by signing a decree that prohibited freedom of the press and assembly.

Fearing a communist uprising, Hindenburg signed another decree, giving Hitler even more power. Persons considered the Nazis' enemies were rounded up and sent to detention centers, or "concentration camps," where torture, slave labor, and executions were secretly carried out. Those who were able to, fled Germany and sought asylum in other countries.

When elections were held on March 5, 1933, the Nazis received 288 seats in the legislature. Now the path was clear to put a final end to the democratic system of the Weimar Republic.

One figure stood in the way of the end of the republic — Hindenburg. Hindenburg had to be convinced of Hitler's loyalty as a German. Hitler had to show the conservative general and his supporters that the Nazi party would serve the national interest.

On March 21 a ceremony was held in a church in Potsdam, a small town just outside of Berlin. Standing beside the grave of Frederick the Great, the 18th-century king of Prussia, Hitler gave a speech. He praised Hindenburg and presented himself as the heir to Hindenburg's legacy. Hindenburg had fought for Germany in the crisis of World War I, and, Hitler claimed, he was fighting for Germany in the crisis of 1933. Then Hitler addressed Hindenburg directly. "By a unique upheaval, national honor has been restored in a few weeks, and, thanks to your understanding, General Field Marshal, the marriage has been consummated between the symbols of the old greatness and the new strength. We pay you homage. A protective providence places you above the new forces of our nation." When Hitler was finished, he walked across the platform and grabbed Hindenburg's hand. The moment was captured by photographers and spread throughout Germany. Hindenburg, representing the old Germany of the empire, appeared to pass power on to the new Germany of Hitler.

On March 23 the Reichstag of Germany effectively abolished itself by passing the Enabling Act. The act shifted the power to pass laws from the legislature to Chancellor Hitler. Hitler's government also

UPI/BETTMANN NEWSPHOTOS

had the power to change the constitution, and soon the Reichstag had no power. Only the Social Democrats, led by Otto Wels, dared to vote against the Enabling Act. Communist delegates were either in concentration camps or in hiding. Hindenburg might still have believed that Hitler would keep his promise. The president of the republic had given his formal support to an extremist radical devoted to destroying democracy.

Immediately after his appointment of Hitler as chancellor, Hindenburg saw what life would be like in Nazi Germany. Hitler's opponents were sent to concentration camps. Attacks on Jews became increasingly violent, and the Nazis called for a boycott of Jewish-owned stores on April 1. Many Jewish shops were smashed. On April 7 the government excluded Jews and certain political groups from government employment. In June the Social Democratic party was banned. By July 14 another law decreed that the Nazis were the only legal political party.

Hindenburg had retreated to his childhood home, Neudeck, near Posen. The estate had been purchased by a group of wealthy landowners and industrialists and presented to Hindenburg as a gift in 1927. In either Neudeck or in Berlin, Hindenburg

With Hitler as chancellor, German socialists, including former Prussian Premier Otto Braun, were taken to concentration camps beginning in August 1933. The cunning right-wing Chancellor Papen of the Center party had sought to exclude the Social Democrats from the German government and convinced Hindenburg to remove socialists from government in Prussia.

The 86-year-old President Hindenburg with his grandchildren in December 1933. Already Hitler's powers were increasing because of another decree signed by Hindenburg, whose fear of communists was played upon by the Nazis. Jews, socialists, and communists were arrested by police, then under Nazi authority.

remained outside of politics and made no effort to resist the transformation of Germany that Hitler was undertaking.

On June 30, 1934, Hitler decided it was time to remove many of his remaining political opponents. For three days executions took place throughout Germany — mainly of rivals and opponents in the Nazi party, including the head of the storm troopers. In Berlin, many of the executions took place in the courtyard of the former Cadet Corps, where Hindenburg had finished his military training more than half a century earlier. Hindenburg did not protest. He sent Hitler a message saying that the dictator had "saved Germany from serious danger." On July 25 the chancellor of Austria was killed by Nazi assassins. This attack and the earlier executions had raised concern about Hitler both in Germany and abroad. It was the last chance to block his consolidation of power. Hindenburg remained silent.

At the age of 86, Hindenburg died on August 2, 1934. He was buried four days later in a major pub-

UPI/BETTMANN NEWSPHOTOS

lic ceremony at Tannenberg. It had been at Tannenberg that the legend of Hindenburg had begun 20 years before: the military hero, the loyal defender of his country.

By turning over the reins of power to Adolf Hitler, Hindenburg unwittingly had set Germany on a spiraling course of fascism, war, and destruction. The Nazis went on to massacre millions of innocent men, women, and children in gas chambers and concentration camps, and in 1939 Hitler began World War II with the invasion of Poland. It would take six years, and countless lives would be shattered or lost, before Germany's Nazi-led mission of ruthless world conquest would finally be defeated. With this defeat, the unified Germany, for which Hindenburg had fought all his life, came to an end. Germany was divided into two states, West Germany (the Federal Republic of Germany) and communist East Germany (the German Democratic Republic), part of Soviet-dominated Eastern Europe.

Hitler speaks at Hindenburg's funeral at Tannenberg. Hindenburg, who died on August 2, 1934, had once written to the Nazi leader that he could not appoint him chancellor, because ". . . a cabinet led by you would force its way to a . . . dictatorship." By 1934, Hitler was Nazi Germany's absolute dictator; German democracy had been destroyed. World War II, launched by Hitler, was five years away.

Further Reading

Goldsmith, Margaret and Frederick Voight. *Hindenburg: The Man and the Legend.* Freeport, N.Y.: Books for Libraries Press, 1972.

Joll, James. *The Origins of the First World War.* New York: Longman Group, 1985.

Kitchen, Martin. *The Silent Dictatorship: The Politics of the German High Command under Hindenburg and Ludendorff, 1916–1918.* London: Croom Helm, 1976.

Laqueur, Walter. *Weimar: A Cultural History 1918–1933.* New York: G. P. Putnam's Sons, 1974.

Taylor, A. J. P. *The Struggle for Mastery in Europe 1848–1918.* New York: Oxford University Press, 1986.

Tuchman, Barbara W. *The Guns of August.* New York: Macmillan Publishing Co., Inc., 1962.

Watt, Richard M. *The Kings Depart, The Tragedy of Germany: Versailles and the German Revolution.* New York: Simon and Schuster, 1968.

Chronology

Oct. 2, 1847	Born Paul Ludwig Hans Anton von Beneckendorff und von Hindenburg in Posen, East Prussia
1859	Hindenburg enters the Cadet Corps
April 1866	Graduates from the Cadet Corps; is made second lieutenant and joins the Third Prussian Guard Regiment
July 3, 1866	Commands the capture of an Austrian battery at the Battle of Königgrätz
1870–71	Serves in the Franco-Prussian War
Jan. 18, 1871	Represents his regiment at the Proclamation of the German Empire at Versailles
1873–77	Attends the Military Academy in Berlin
1878	Promoted to the army's general staff
1897	Promoted to major general
1903	Appointed commanding general of the Fourth Army Corps
1911	Retires from active service
June 28, 1914	Assassination of Austrian Archduke Franz Ferdinand
Aug. 1914	Germany declares war on Russia; beginning of World War I
Aug. 22, 1914	Hindenburg recalled to active service as commander in chief of the troops fighting Russia
Aug. 26–30, 1914	Commands the German victory at the Battle of Tannenberg
Nov. 1914	Promoted to field marshal
May 7, 1915	German submarine sinks the British ocean liner *Lusitania*
Aug. 29, 1916	Hindenburg becomes the chief of the army's general staff
Nov. 1918	German is declared a republic; Kaiser Wilhelm II flees the country Armistice ends World War I
July 4, 1919	Hindenburg returns to retirement
March 1920	Royalist soldiers stage the unsuccessful Kapp putsch
April 26, 1925	Hindenburg is elected president
1930	Signs the Young Plan, which removes last foreign troops from Germany and sets schedule for war reparation payments
April 10, 1932	Reelected president
July 20, 1932	Approves the federal takeover of the left-wing government in Prussia
Jan. 30, 1933	Appoints Adolf Hitler chancellor
Feb. 4, 1933	Signs a decree limiting freedoms of press and assembly
March 23, 1933	The Reichstag passes the Enabling Act, the foundation for Hitler's dictatorship
Aug. 2, 1934	Hindenburg dies at 86 years of age

Index

Russell A. Berman is Associate Professor of German Studies at Stanford University. His interests include modern German culture and politics as well as literature and literary theory. He has published articles and books in these areas, including *The Rise of the Modern German Novel: Crisis and Charisma.*

Arthur M. Schlesinger, jr., taught history at Harvard for many years and is currently Albert Schweitzer Professor of the Humanities at City University of New York. He is the author of numerous highly praised works in American history and has twice been awarded the Pulitzer Prize. He served in the White House as special assistant to Presidents Kennedy and Johnson.